ADAM TORRES

PRESENTS

VOLUME 1

CULTURAL
EDITION

I0123416

DIVERSITY
MATTERS

Top Asian Leaders Share Their Views on
EQUALITY AND INCLUSION

FEATURED AUTHORS:

Alexander Eng	Japman Bajaj
Alice Yi	Jeneviere Kim
Ban Tran	Jessie Wang
Chirag Sagar	Minji Chang
Christine Drinan	Neil Yeoh
Eva Iino	Shaan Patel
Hanna Li	Stella Song

INTRODUCTION BY
CHIRAG SAGAR

CENTURY
CITY

Century City, CA

ENTER TO
WIN PRIZES
from *Money Matters* Top Tips

Scan the QR Code for entry into the contest.

WIN HERE

Follow Money Matters Top Tips to learn from other entrepreneurs, executives, and business owners on how to become a thought-leader in your field.

Podcast: **www.MoneyMattersTopTips.com/Podcast**
Instagram: **www.instagram.com/moneymatterstoptips**
Subscribe to the blog: **www.MoneyMattersTopTips.com**
Facebook: **www.facebook.com/moneymatterstoptips**
Twitter: **www.twitter.com/moneymatterstop**

Contest subject to terms and conditions listed on website.
No purchase necessary to participate.

For information, visit **www.MrCenturyCity.com**

Edited by:
Adam Torres

Graphic Design:
Kendra Cagle

MONEY
MATTERS

Century City, CA 90067
www.MrCenturyCity.com

The Mr. Century City Logo is a trademark of Mr. Century City, LLC.

ISBN-13: 978-1-949680-15-7

Money Matters, Beverly Hills, CA

DEDICATION

To the people who struggle to make
equality and inclusion a reality.

TABLE OF CONTENTS

ACKNOWLEDGEMENTS

Special thanks to Chirag Sagar and his team. Their vision
for this project is what helped make it a reality.

I would also like to thank the following individuals
for their support and hard work.

Stella Song, CEO of Destination Luxury

Alice Yi, Esq.

Michael Douglas Carlin, Editor, Century City News

Megan Kimble, Editor

Kendra Cagle, 5 Lakes Design

Christine Lee

Christopher Kai, KGL Consulting

Kris Lee, MD

FOREWORD

By **ADAM TORRES**

Benjamin Franklin was one of my great inspirations in becoming a writer, publishing books, and getting involved with diverse forms of media to effect change. His use of the printing press and its power to use words to disseminate ideas inspired me to do the same. Through writing, he educated people which created real change. This education was part of what led to the early colonies gaining their independence and creating the free United States of America that I am proud to call home. Since its inception, the U.S. has served as a home for immigrants and a type of "melting pot" that has allowed cultures to learn from each other and to connect.

As the U.S. matures and the generations accumulate, differences can become less obvious and the lines between cultures blur. In cities like Los Angeles, it is common to eat cuisine and sample dishes from cultures around the world just by traveling a few miles or blocks. During this new era of hyper-connectivity, it's important to recognize and celebrate the cultures that collectively make us whole. Recognizing our differences in order to gain a better sense of understanding of everyone serves as a basis for moving us forward as a society.

This is what the "Diversity Matters" series is all about. My previous books have focused primarily on business-related topics such as finance and real estate. But when Chirag Sagar came to me with the idea to create a book focused on diversity, I couldn't pass it up. It was an opportunity to relate with people on a very real level through sharing their personal stories and getting to the heart of what makes up the fabric of an individual's DNA. My books have always been designed to spark conversation and the exchange of ideas. These books will complement and further that mission in a meaningful way that I hope can effect change.

To the authors that have participated in this inaugural edition of "Diversity Matters," I am grateful. I am grateful that they were willing to be vulnerable, share their stories, and serve as role models as the topic of inclusion and diversity becomes more prevalent, especially as the world becomes increasingly connected and societies merge.

To the readers who are embarking on this journey, I ask that you maintain an open mind. Some of the stories you encounter may be foreign to your personal experience, while others you may readily identify with. Stick with the ideas that don't at first make sense to you and seek out further understanding by sparking conversations with your peers. Remember, the goal of this book is to keep the conversation around diversity going. To battle for attention among the countless other things that are vying for your time. It's important that we maintain our sensitivity and not become numb to the topic.

And if you have stories about business or diversity you would like to share, connect with me on Instagram at @AskAdamTorres

With appreciation,

Adam Torres

INTRODUCTION

By CHIRAG SAGAR

It all started with an email.

"The University of Southern California and Warner Bros. Pictures invite you and a guest to attend a special screening of Crazy Rich Asians. Following the screening, there will be a Q&A with Director SCA Alumnus Jon M. Chu and Warner Bros. Chairman & CEO/USC Alumnus Kevin Tsujihara."

I forwarded the email to my girlfriend and asked her if she'd like to attend. She replied with an emphatic "YES!" because she too is an Asian American actress. It seemed like a great date night, and I RSVP'd immediately.

USC is my alma mater. I'm a proud Board of Director serving on the university's Asian Pacific Alumni Association. When USC partnered with Warner Bros. Pictures to share this film with students and alumni, the Asian Pacific Alumni Association was one of the main proponents of promoting the movie to the university's constituents.

When my girlfriend and I arrived at USC, we could feel the buzz in the air. There was a line with hundreds of people waiting to see the film that wrapped around the theatre. Well over capacity, USC turned away several hundred guests. Oddly enough, even those turned away were enthused to be a part of such a positive response to seeing the film. I didn't realize the movie had received so much publicity and built so much buzz until I got there and saw the madness that ensued to get our seats. At that point, I was unaware of the significance of the film—the first time an all-Asian cast was assembled for a major Hollywood film since Joy Luck Club came out more than 25 years ago.

During the Q&A session between John M. Chu and Kevin Tsujiara, it became clear that this fact was instrumental for so many individuals in the room. Many of the attendees of Asian descent could relate to the actor's stories and dilemma. It was an inspirational moment for everyone, including me. Crazy Rich Asians went on to become a major blockbuster success. I went home that evening curious to learn more about how Asian Americans are viewed in the media and entertainment space.

I dug into research about how Asian and Asian Americans are underrepresented in leadership positions in virtually every industry. This wasn't just an entertainment and media problem—it was common across the board in many industries. I shared my findings with the publisher of my last book, Adam Torres, and told him about some personal stories related to what it was like growing up as an Asian American in Los Angeles. I mentioned it would be great to be able to write a book on this. He surprised me when he said that's exactly what we needed to do.

Digging deeper, I chatted with several others who shared their frustrations about this topic with me. I realized there was an opportunity to address diversity and inclusion issues facing many companies, governments, nonprofits, and more. People we spoke to about the book understood what we were doing and asked how they could be involved to help us tackle diversity issues. We saw this as a vital opportunity to share stories to create more diversity in many industries, and also provide examples of inclusion. What started as a personal frustration, evolved into sparking the idea for this book.

As the result of this effort, I bring you 14 authors, including men and women in more than 11 cities and more than a dozen industries with varying backgrounds, spanning a couple of generations, sharing their stories to help us all progress. We hope this book inspires you further to tackle diversity and create a more inclusive world.

Thank you,

Chirag Sagar

CHAPTER 1

BUILDING RELATIONSHIPS TO STRENGTHEN OUR COMMUNITY

By **ALEXANDER ENG**

We sat huddled around the TV waiting for that famous ball to drop in New York's Time Square. Five, four, three, two, one--"Happy New Year!" Screams filled the room as everyone welcomed the coming year. American New Years was always an exciting time for me. It was a holiday that reminded me I was different from many of my friends. Sure, I did many of the things my friends did, like playing baseball, soccer, fishing, and skiing. I also benefited from being raised in a hospitality-driven family that was very connected to our community. But being raised as a Chinese American in the small Pacific Northwestern town of Pullman, Washington, had its downsides. Although there wasn't much cultural diversity there, I never saw this as a negative, as the community always embraced and supported me and my family without hesitation. Growing up, being different from others actually provided a great benefit that taught me many of the values that guide me today, both in my personal and business life. These lessons would not come in a classroom setting. Instead, I learned through experience.

My great-grandfather, Charlie Eng, immigrated to the United States in the late 1800s to work on the railroads in San Francisco. As he worked his way up from a laborer to a house servant, he ended up in the Pacific Northwest, where he saved enough money to open a small Chinese restaurant. This restaurant represented the nucleus of our family and was passed down to my grandfather and eventually to my father and uncle. Although I was raised in an agriculturally influenced environment, because our family owned a restaurant, I spent a lot of time in the business and hospitality space. I like to say I have "business in my blood." I learned at an early age that a restaurant could be a special place: A conduit of sorts, where people come for more than just food or to satisfy their hunger-- they also come for the experience of community, to be enveloped by love, to share experiences and conversations with people they know, and to forge new friendships.

Our restaurant served as an anchor for my family and for our wonderful community as well. Most of my family, including myself, have worked or helped out at some point. More importantly, this restaurant was a cornerstone for a growing Chinese community in Pullman. One of the first lessons my family taught me was the importance of developing a network. In the early 1900s, many families in Pacific Northwest and across the West Coast worked to help their friends and family still in Southeastern China to immigrate to the United States. In our family, we helped people from our village get to the United States and gain employment. Some worked in my family's restaurant, while others pursued alternative avenues of work. Once they were here, it was essential to help them get their families here. Often, husbands were separated from their wives and children. They had to work hard to get them here which required time and money. This idea of helping one another for the greater good of the community transcends cultural boundaries.

Understanding this spirit of community helped to drive the Chinese American business and civic environment. The Eng Family Association was also born out of this concept. By nature of my last name (Eng), I was born into this organization, taking my place alongside my ancestors. I was taught what networking was at an early age and about the exponential impact those connections could create. We helped by supporting one another, through connecting our respective family and business networks together. People gathered, all with the last name Eng, and connected about exchanging ideas, telling their stories, and supporting each other's dreams. Echoes of people saying, "How can I help?" could be heard during the meetings. We had the common goal of supporting and creating a vibrant and culturally significant family and business community. Everyone within the Eng Association brought their expertise to benefit those within the community. On the hospitality side, our expertise was simple: We fed people. Because food is the universal connector of all industries and commerce, if someone was in town and needed a place to stay, we arranged accommodations and sometimes a job or two for them, while others in the family helped with their specialties. We discovered that we were stronger united and built a community that prospered by working together.

Today, when I think about what globalization and social media have done to unite people, it amazes me. Pullman is home to Washington State University and in recent years, it has gained more of an international feel. When I grew up celebrating the Chinese New Year, I didn't know that how many other people also celebrated this holiday. There was no Google or YouTube available to watch these traditions around the world. Very few of my friends at school celebrated the holiday. I didn't know the extent of how other people celebrated the holiday. A majority of the Asian Americans I knew growing up were fellow Eng family members.

Attending the University of Southern California was the next step in my journey. In Los Angeles, a whole new world of connectivity opened to me. I can celebrate with many others linked by a common tradition and heritage. I still remember my first Chinese New Year celebration in Los Angeles. We went out to a Chinese restaurant, and I was able to see many others celebrating what once seemed like something only my family did.

In college, my horizons expanded. Coming from a small town to a large city was somewhat of a cultural awakening. I was exposed to a tremendous amount of diversity that helped me to understand my heritage, but it also taught me to cherish the values I developed growing up in a small town. After college, it was time for me to enter the "real world." My first position after graduation was as a pharmaceutical representative. One of the most exciting things about this position was when I realized that some companies hire to reflect the markets they serve. For example, my territory in Los

Angeles was culturally diverse but predominately Asian. This made a lot of sense because it allowed me to connect with the clientele on a cultural level. But speaking the same language did not guarantee success. In fact, my grandfather's lesson of creating a network was essential as I worked to become successful in the role. Developing a sound network and cultivating those relationships would be crucial to my future success.

In my territory, I was to develop relationships with the doctors and other medical professionals in order to grow our business. A common business development practice was holding dinners for the doctors. These were educational events and featured curated speakers. The idea was to support the medical community through education, to demonstrate that we would continue to provide resources going forward. Seems simple enough, right? I quickly learned otherwise. I thought everything was going well with one of the events that I was responsible for. We had many RSVPs prior to the event. However, when the day arrived, few people actually attended. This was a problem. How could we develop relationships and further our business interests if we were speaking to an empty room? I had to go back to my roots, to think like I was trained to think since childhood. The first course of action was to seek out influencers in the medical community that were also leaders in civic causes. Next, I worked on deepening relationships by supporting causes and initiatives both I and the influencers believed were important. What were the philanthropic efforts they cared about? How could I support and serve them? How are they aligned with the causes we as a company support? I wanted to develop a sense of community like the one I experienced in Pullman growing up.

It took some time, but by partnering with the right influencers in the communities we were targeting, our business grew and we were able to create meaningful partnerships that met the objectives of all parties involved. But I was ready for my next challenge. The opportunity to see such an interesting industry up close created a desire to learn more about other industries. This pursuit led me to the field of banking. Transitioning into the world of banking from pharmaceutical sales gave me the opportunity to take my community-building efforts to the next level. Historically, U.S.-based banks have often lost out on serving local Asian clientele as they banked with smaller, more culturally focused regional banks. Immigrants and first-generation Asians typically supported regional banks because they felt like these institutions were set up to better understand them. The perception was that small meant working with someone more relatable, not necessarily because of the products or resources they offered. This was due to a deficit in Cultural Intelligence (CQ) by large U.S. banks. CQ goes beyond existing notions of cultural sensitivity. An organization with a high level of CQ is not only aware of cultural differences, but it can also work and relate with people across different cultural contexts.

I believe the Asian American community can have the best of both worlds. The old days of a lack of connectivity between a big bank and its potential Asian clientele are over. A bank can have both a high CQ and the resources of a large institution. This is exactly what my team and I execute daily. I'm privileged to have the support of leaders who not only embrace CQ, but also live CQ through their actions. We are finding that the next generation prefers to partner with a bank that will make investments in technology, infrastructure, and resources. But they still want to be understood. They want individuals that speak their language and work with a team that follows their culture and traditions. This move in banking is part of a more significant paradigm shift that is taking place in business across many fields. No longer do banks tell their customers, "this is what you should know." Now, they say, "this is what you should know, but more importantly, this is the context in which you should know it in." I think this is great for inclusion and diversity going forward.

Another shift that is taking place in terms of diversity is the hiring practices of corporate America. Large corporations realize that a diverse workforce that is representative of the communities they are serving is good business. Being dynamic and focused, my bank is able to deliver our services not only with a regional bank feel, but also with a remarkable amount of resources that only can be found in a large bank. If you want to put a bank branch in the middle of an Asian neighborhood, the associates working there will have to speak the languages found within the community and understand the culture. If they don't, it will be difficult for them to connect to the local clientele. Historically within the banking industry, Asian Americans were predominantly found in support roles rather than management. While there is always room for improvement, the industry is definitely changing. More and more Asian Americans can be seen reflecting the communities that they serve by being on frontline in client-facing roles. This trend will make for a stronger, more vibrant banking community in the long-term. In a commodity-driven industry such as banking, diversity-focused hiring practices can make an incredible difference.

As I've experienced both the Chinese New Year and the American New Year, I've realized the American New Year is often centered around resolutions. What was accomplished last year? What wasn't? Were you trying to lose weight or land that new job? If it didn't happen, is this the year? Popular media and advertising often put pressure on what can be accomplished in the coming year, making for a hectic season. One part of the Chinese New Year that I think everyone can learn from is its focus on family and the community. Instead of huddling around a TV, we circle a table and talk over bountiful amounts of food. Food, as it turns out, connects us with our past and our future by creating a time for us to pause and reflect. It's the same as good old-fashioned Pullman-style talking. Our family learns and grows together, strengthening our familial bonds. Chinese New Year is about being thankful for the past year's successes, failures, and the lessons learned through experiencing them. Gratitude permeates everything in this season of renewal. Be thankful for what you received this past year, but embrace change and uncertainty knowing you must act to improve things for the next generation. This provides the foundation that fuses the Eastern and Western cultures together through optimism.

CHAPTER 2

MY WAY HOME

By **ALICE YI**

DIVERSITY: the condition of having or being composed of differing elements: VARIETY

especially: the inclusion of different types of people (such as people of different races or cultures) in a group or organization.

(Merriam-Webster)

Over the years my understanding and appreciation of the word "diversity" has evolved along with my life experiences. I learned the textbook definition of diversity in a school setting as a child. I knew it to be a buzzword of sorts, the kind of word praised by many around me. Back then, it was just one of many words that we needed to learn in school, but over time the word diversity would eventually become very significant to me.

Growing up as a daughter of two Korean immigrants in Southern California, I was surrounded from the very earliest parts of my upbringing by a great variety of people from different ethnicities and cultures. My parents came to the United States with very little money, and landed in Hollywood, California, to start their version of the American dream. I lived in a tiny one-bedroom apartment with my parents, older sister, and younger brother. When I was about three years old, we moved to the suburbs of Los Angeles and we lived in a neighborhood with a great mix people from different races and cultures. Many of those neighborhood children attended the same elementary school as my younger brother and me and it was normal to us that our friends were Caucasian, Asian, African American, and Latino. We played youth sports with kids from many backgrounds and, while the population in our area was predominantly Caucasian, there was always a significant representation of minorities in most of the activities we did.

When I think back on my time growing up in Southern California, I remember instances of racism directed toward me or toward my family. Some of the kids at school would make fun of my Asian eyes or sneeringly call me "ching chong." Although they were rare instances, I still recall feeling like an outsider. This behavior was frowned upon in my school and social activities. When our school held its annual "Unity Day" program to remind students of the virtues of diversity, I felt like it was an unnecessary waste of time. It seemed as though everyone was repeatedly stating the obvious: Be kind to each other and embrace our differences. As a child I didn't really see the point of hammering this one sentiment into all of our minds.

When I was a child, my dad worked at improving his English skills and getting his real estate brokers license. Among our friends and the families we knew, he was known as someone people could turn to whenever they needed help deciphering quasi-legal documents. Some of the matters were related to real estate but many others were just documents that required translation or general advice. One day our neighbor's grandfather came to my dad asking for immediate assistance. He had received a letter from the Social Security office stating that all of his benefits would be revoked shortly. There was insufficient explanation for this decision and my dad was determined to help his friend. They traveled through rush hour traffic to get to the Social Security office and waited hours for their turn. My dad pleaded with the officials there to reverse the decision that revoked his friend's benefits and was repeatedly told that there was nothing they could do to help him. Undeterred, they returned the following day, traveling through traffic and waiting in line. Once again they were turned away. My dad said it seemed as though no one they spoke to had the authority or understanding to assist them. They were told that there was no one in the office who could reverse the decision, yet my dad insisted that denying his friend all of his benefits was a ludicrous and wrong conclusion. The following day, they traveled yet again back to the Social Security office through traffic and endured another long wait. When it was finally their turn, my dad demanded to speak to someone who could help them.

The case escalated to the highest manager in the office. My dad explained the whole situation again. The manager was dumbfounded at what had happened. She read through the file and immediately reinstated all of our neighbor's previously revoked benefits. It was an incredible relief for our neighbor and he was grateful for my dad's assistance. My dad was only happy to help.

He often told me this story to encourage me to go to law school. He said that with a law degree, I would be able to accomplish what he did in three long visits to the Social Security office with one phone call or letter. It was at this time that I started to think that perhaps someday I could become an attorney.

In high school, I was a typical teenage girl, spending much of my time playing volleyball. I was as focused on improving my skills as an athlete as much as I was on schoolwork and was eventually rewarded with an opportunity to enroll at Wellesley College and play on the volleyball team. A liberal arts college for women located near Boston, Massachusetts, Wellesley is a school that prides itself on the diversity of its faculty and students. It truly is a haven for people of all backgrounds. I enjoyed learning in a classroom environment that highly encouraged open discussion with people from countries around the world. Upon graduation, I attended the London School of Economics and Political Science to earn a Master's Degree in Public Policy and Philosophy. Although this school and indeed the city of London was a very cosmopolitan place with students and residents from many different cultures, during my time in London, I found myself facing more racism from people on the streets than I had ever faced in my more than 20 years living in the United States. I found it absurd but I could brush it off as the action of ignorant strangers.

When I decided to go to law school, I applied to many schools across the nation and narrowed it down to three. I ended up choosing the University of Minnesota in Minneapolis. Not only does it have an excellent academic reputation, but I also found the people I met on my campus visit very friendly. I could easily envision myself loving life in the Twin Cities. I packed up my things and moved to Minneapolis to start the next chapter of my life.

I was surprised to realize that it was by far the least diverse school I had ever attended. It was the least diverse community I had ever lived in. It was odd to find myself among a large population and feel like part of a small minority. I learned that there is a population of Asians who were adopted as children from Korea and China living in and around the Twin Cities. People would often see me and assume that I must be one of the Korean adoptees. This I didn't mind much but it reinforced the feeling that I didn't blend in--that people saw me as an "other." I'd speak with two of my female friends, also minorities, and they expressed similar feelings of not fitting in and of being self-conscious about being an Asian woman in the Midwest. I found myself wondering how much it affected the way people saw me, whether it impacted my relationships, or my opportunities for career advancement. It may very well be the case that being Asian in the Midwest had no impact whatsoever on these things, but I found myself, for the first time in my life, wondering whether I truly "fit in." These seeds of doubt were overpowered by the loveliness of the Twin Cities -the beautiful running trails along the many lakes and the Mississippi River and the close-knit circle of friends I made there. Although I sometimes forgot the doubts I had, there was a lingering feeling of unease that I had all throughout my time there.

After graduation, I had the privilege to work with many different judges for a handful of years at the District Court in Saint Paul,

Minnesota. There, I was able to witness and assist the legal process in the courtroom setting. I was able to get an incredible sense of the complex mechanisms of the court system. It was the experience of a lifetime to be able to work on a variety of different criminal and civil legal matters, learning from accomplished attorneys and judges.

Once, I was working on a project in which I shared a room with many different attorneys. People would often break up the silence with stories or jokes to pass the time. I befriended a woman who sat by me. She and I were part of the quieter bunch of the group. One day an older man spoke up, clearly eager to retell a joke he had told before. I wasn't there when he told it the first time and wanted to hear what he was going to say. As he started into the story, my friend abruptly told him not to repeat the joke. It was uncharacteristic of her to behave in this way--I was stunned by her comments. An awkward silence followed. My colleagues insisted that the man continue and he started his story once more. Once again, my friend firmly told him to stop. Now I was more confused than ever. Again, he was encouraged to tell the story, as many people hadn't heard it earlier. Over my friend's loud protests he finally did tell the story, a story playing up on overtly racist stereotypes of Asians. I was in utter shock.

After he told the story, I was shocked. I couldn't believe that someone would find it appropriate to tell such a joke in a work environment. But there were many things to learn from this experience. After the initial shock wore off, I felt grateful to my friend who didn't mind looking like a fool in front of our colleagues in an effort to shield me from the ignorant jokester. I think about how lucky I am to know someone who would instinctively stand up for me in that way. Also, looking at the man and the situation in retrospect, I wouldn't label him a racist. He told an offensive joke directed at people like me, but his heart isn't hateful. I can't say that he was purposefully attacking me. I can only explain it as him not being socially aware by assuming that everyone shares his sense of humor.

I'm not saying that this was a common experience in Minnesota or that something like this couldn't happen in California, Massachusetts, or London--it just never happened to me in these places. Moreover, I understand that when I'm living in a diverse community, I'm much more confident in myself and such instances have a much smaller impact on me. I have very fond memories of my time in Minnesota. I have an enormous amount of love and gratitude to the people I met there. I made some of my dearest friends in the Twin Cities and accomplished some of my greatest life goals there. Not for a moment do I regret choosing to live in the Midwest.

I eventually made my way back to Southern California, a place where I feel most comfortable. Looking back at my life's journey, I realize how fortunate I have been to live in communities and cities around the world with ample diversity. But it was incredibly important for my development to live in a place with a lesser degree of diversity. I don't like to admit that I took living in such diverse places for granted, that living away from it really made me realize how vital it is for my happiness and for my growth as a person. But it's true. I knew that I was fortunate before, but I suppose I didn't see how very truly blessed I was for it. I'm grateful that my parents raised us to bond with people of other cultures, and how it was no accident that we grew up in our part of Southern California. I know

now how programs like "Unity Day" serve as an important reminder to celebrate our differences and I can appreciate the efforts of those before me who prioritized the importance of diversity. I credit these programs and the people behind them for laying the down the foundation to be kind to each other and embrace our differences.

In the era of Black Lives Matter, I haven't suffered the serious injustices that others have experienced, but I do feel people in all communities benefit from exposure to and acceptance of people from all backgrounds. Nowadays, I find myself eager to participate in initiatives that support diversity not only so I can feel accepted but also so I can accept others. One way I choose to support diversity is by collaborating with friends from a group that I belong to of young professionals who enjoy theatre. We are currently creating a new group to encourage people from all cultures to enjoy theatre in the Los Angeles area. We aim to make the theatre-going experience more accessible to people of all circumstances. Our goal is to appeal to and include people from dissimilar socio-economic and ethnic backgrounds.

Professionally, I've discovered that working in a diverse environment allows for more growth and helps eliminate "tunnel vision." Adding more perspectives enables a group to approach tasks from multiple angles, which in turn helps develop creative solutions. It's these kinds of creative, multi-perspective resolutions that I find the most rewarding, making my journey through law school and beyond seem so worthwhile.

My dad continues to help his friends now as he did before. Now I often help him address the legal matters that arise. And just as he once predicted, sometimes I can indeed help solve some of their problems with just one phone call or letter.

CHAPTER 3

FOLLOWING YOUR CALLING:
It's Not Easy, But It's Well Worth It

By **BAN TRAN**

As I am sitting here, I realize that I have less than two weeks to complete the business plan for my media blockchain technology joint-venture. I also have to write my presentation speech on nanotechnology and the application of graphene for social impact for when I'll be addressing 15 ambassadors and a President from a country in Africa, whom will be arriving in New York City for the United Nations General Assembly.

You could say that my lifestyle is not normal. The path that led me here is one filled with adventures, hardships, and invaluable lessons learned. As difficult as it may have seemed at the time,

I recognize now how crucial each phase of my life has been in molding my character. I am grateful that I learned the importance of self-reflection during these difficulties, which helped me develop strategic resolutions. I hope the story of my struggles to break barriers as an Asian American immigrant will inspire others to follow their dreams, tackle challenges, and recognize that adversities will serve to aid them in embracing their destiny.

I am an international business entrepreneur with a background in international business, private equity, technology, and politics. I have a private holding company in New York City with equities in multiple business sectors, which include supply chain management, infrastructure development, international business advisory, and disruptive technologies. On the technology side, I am also a partner in a technology lab in Irvine, California, where I work with a team of biotech, nuclear physics, and quantum physics scientists from Harvard, MIT, Caltech, Stanford, John Hopkins, University of Pennsylvania, UC Berkeley, UC Irvine, USC, and Rice University, along with other strategic partners to develop some of the most comprehensive technological solutions for society's challenges. I particularly focus on nanotechnology, blockchain, artificial intelligence, and big data. My role is to commercialize the technologies that are matured for social impact and industrial applications.

Sometimes it all sounds overwhelming, but I can assure you that I did not follow a life plan to end up where I am today. My ethnicity is a mixture of Chinese and Vietnamese. My family emigrated from Vietnam to the U.S. in 1990 when I was 8 years old and I grew up in a working-class family in an Asian community in San Gabriel, a small town on the outskirts of Los Angeles. I was sheltered most of my life, trying to get by without getting into any trouble.

Fitting in was a big challenge for me when we first arrived in the United States due to cultural differences and the language barrier. Kids can be cruel, especially when you pick your nose in public. Like many young immigrants, I was subjected to bullying and name-calling due to my ignorance and cultural idiosyncrasies. Luckily, I was a quick learner and I was able to adapt in less than a year. I learned during this process that the best way to foster acceptance is through communication and shared values, which come from common belief and shared interests. For example, at the time, the kids in my class were into marbles. I was good at it and earned their respect by being one of the best marble players in school. Although my relationships with these kids were mostly superficial, I understood that in order to avoid creating enemies, I would have to blend in by dressing and talking like them. Little did I know at the time, but this was my first real-life lesson in politics, which would play a crucial role in aiding me in my future business career.

During my freshman and sophomore years in high school, I was still caught up in trying to fit in and did not pay attention to my grades. Although I worked hard during my junior and senior years to make it up, my overall GPA was still too low to qualify for any scholarship. To make matter worse, my parents combined household income was just slightly too high for me to quality for financial aid, which meant that we would have to pay for my entire college education out of pocket. Although my parents could not afford it, not going to college was not an option. So my parents took out loans to put me through college and tried to figure out how to pay for it later. They wanted me to become either a doctor, a lawyer, or an engineer. Since I could not stand blood and found the law to be dull, I decided to study Electrical and Computer Engineering (ECE). It was a popular major, as we were at the peak of the dot-com boom.

A year and a half into college, the dot-com bubble burst. Internet companies were folding one after another, and what had seemed to me like a stable career path shattered in an instant. This experience taught me how quickly industries come and go. If I wanted to have control over my future, I would have to venture beyond learning just technical skills and study the the cycles themselves, learning both about economics and people. Because I came from a working-class family, there was no one to guide me. Both my parents were timid people who could barely speak English. I knew that to become the person I wanted to be, I would have to figure it out on my own. I did everything I could to expose myself to new things, from meeting different kinds of people to joining social clubs to participating in a multilevel marketing company. Although it was an unconventional path, I saw joining a marketing company as a platform for me to meet new people and learn the fundamentals of sales. I stuck with it to learn what I could and then moved on to other ventures once I had outgrown the environment.

As I experimented with entrepreneurship and reflected what I wanted my career path to be, I felt the need to go out and explore the world to gain more perspectives. I knew then that I was not meant to be an employee, so I began to think about dropping out of school--even though I knew that my parents would never allow it to happen. I felt guilty putting my parents into so much debt while I studied a discipline I had no interest in. I was still stuck in this dilemma when I finished my second year of college. When a couple of old high school friends decided to visit the East Coast for the summer, I took that opportunity to break out of the San Gabriel-bubble and explore the world.

I was a broke college student, so I sold whatever I could on eBay to save up for my trip. I managed to earn enough to purchase my plane ticket with $200 to spare to spend during my trip. I told my parents I would be going on vacation to the East Coast, but I already knew that once I arrived, I would stay--I would attempt to survive and figure it out on my own. I never asked my parents for any assistance because I knew that they would never permit me to go if they knew my plans. I was a just a naïve young boy venturing out into the world without a sound strategy.

I landed in Boston's Logan International Airport on September 10, 2002. My old high school friends, Son and Andy, who had flown in a week earlier, picked me up from the airport. We spent the next couple days hanging out and catching up in Boston and then headed out to New York City.

Once we arrived in New York, I was introduced to Steve, with whom we would stay with during the weekdays, and Bobby, with whom we would stay during the weekends. Although they were both Andy's friends, I noticed a big contrast in their characters and lifestyles. Steve lived with his mother in a public housing project, came from a rough neighborhood, dressed very poorly, and was a penny-pincher. Bobby also lived with his mother and sister, but in a nice house, in a nice neighborhood. He was well-groomed, a lady's man. Coming from a conservative family, I had a bad impression of Steve because of stereotypes I held about [this thing]. His stinginess started getting on my nerves as we continued to hang out.

The tension escalated further when we were coming home from our third night out on the town. My phone had been stolen at a local pool hall and I was feeling distressed. It was nearly midnight and Steve told us he needed to borrow our rental car and that he would be back in 45 minutes. He did not want us to come along with him, yet we were also not allowed into his home without him because his mother was not comfortable with strangers. My friends and I waited on the front steps of his apartment feeling scared and vulnerable. Three hours passed and Steve was nowhere to be found. At this point, I wanted to strangle the guy. Then at 5 a.m., he finally pulled up in our rental car. He apologized and admitted that he went to see his ex-girlfriend and fell asleep. I wanted to punch Steve in the face, but then Son stopped me. He pulled me aside and said, "Ban, I know you don't like Steve and neither do I. But you have to learn to get along with everybody because you never know when you might need them." I wanted to punch Steve so bad, but out of respect for Son, I let it go.

For the rest of the week, we all hung out and had fun exploring what New York City had to offer. Most of the time, I avoided talking to Steve and spent time conversing with Bobby. On our last day together, Steve's stomach growled all morning. I knew he was hungry but that he could not afford to eat. Although we were all broke, I was fortunate because Son and Andy had paid for me whenever we went out to eat. But on the last day, when I went to buy fast food for myself, I decided to buy Steve a cheeseburger as well. He hesitated but then grabbed the cheeseburger.

Finally, the time had come for my friends to go back to California. This was the moment for me to make my big decision: whether to go back or to stay and figure it out on my own. I decided to stay. I worked out a deal to stay with Bobby in Fort Lee, New Jersey until I found my own place. I called my parents from a pay phone to inform them that I would not be coming back. They were furious, but there was nothing they could do because I was already 3,000 miles away from home. Now, it was either sink or swim.

The following week, after I figured out the public transportation system, I went all over the city looking for a job while Bobby was working. Nobody wanted to hire me because I had no experience. I was turned down from even entry-level jobs. The sun was scorching and I suffered from heat exhaustion from being out all day. Only now did I grasp how quickly $200 could disappear. I had to learn to ration. I gave myself a budget of $2 a day for food: a 99-cent burger for lunch and another 99-cent burger for dinner. The bulk of my money would be saved for taking public transportation.

By the end of the week, I was running out of clean clothes. Since Bobby didn't have a washer and dryer, I asked Bobby if I could use the landlord's in the garage. Although he said no at first, Bobby eventually relented and told me to make sure I got it out before the landlord got home. I agreed and proceeded to do my laundry. Unfortunately, I fell asleep while waiting for the laundry to dry. I woke up to Bobby's angry voice. Apparently, Bobby got reprimanded by the landlord for using his washer and dryer. I apologized but Bobby did not want to hear any of it. Consumed with anger, Bobby kicked me out of the house. Still exhausted from the heat, I threw all my clothes into my luggage and walked to the nearest bus stop. It still had not occurred to me how bad of a situation I was in because my mind was still dazed from the lack of sleep. I did not know where to go nor what to do. I was broke, homeless, and I had no cell phone to call anyone.

As I rode the longest bus ride of my life back into New York City, my mind churned. What do I do, where will I sleep, how will I survive? It then occurred to me to reach out to the only person left I knew in New York: Steve. When I got to New York City, it was close to 10 p.m. I called Steve from the nearest pay phone. I let go of any pride I had left, explained to Steve my predicament, and asked him for help. Steve told me that he would get off work at 12 a.m. and told me to meet him at his home in Jackson Heights, Queens.

When I met Steve at his house, he took me around the building to the back where we would enter from the basement level of the projects. There were shoes hanging from electrical wires and graffiti everywhere. We walked through a hallway full of leaks and entered a small room on the basement level covered in cobwebs. As bad as I thought the condition of his home was when we first met, this was much worse. Steve said the upstairs room we had stayed in was his sister's. This was actually his room. Steve told me that his sister was visiting from school for the next three days so there was no room for me at the moment. He would allow me to leave my stuff there, but I would have to figure out where to sleep on my own for the next three days until his sister went back to her dorm. I did not care whether I would have to wander the street for three days, or whether I would be staying in the basement of a housing project. I was just happy that someone had come to my rescue. The statement Son had told me about learning to get along with everybody because you never know when you might need them would forever be ingrained in my head.

From that moment forward, my values were completely changed. Loyalty and integrity had become the top of my priorities, replacing women and cars. For the next three days, I wandered the street, homeless, but I was determined to persevere. I learned the rules of the streets so I would not get myself in trouble. During the day I would wander supermarkets and sit in internet cafés to stay cool from the heat. At night, I would go to 24-hours pool halls, buy a drink, nap for a couple of hours, and rotate to the next location before they kicked me out. I told myself that this was a test from God. How could I expect to be somebody in life if I could not learn to survive on my own? After the third day, I was finally given a roof over my head. Not knowing where the future would take me, I was able to survive by taking it day by day and addressing each challenge as it arose. This experience changed me from a naive boy to a street smart individual.

One month later, I found out another friend from California, Michael, was planning to move out to Boston. We got in touch, I told him what happened, and he agreed to let me stay with him. Words spread back to Son and Andy. They were shocked to hear what I had gone through. They decided to pool together whatever money they had and shipped my car from California, along with pillows, blankets, clothes, and whatever else they could stuff into it. Once I received the car, I thanked Son, Andy, and Steve for their generosity and took off to Boston to meet with Michael. In the coming months,

Michael also aided me by allowing me to live with him rent-free until I was able to get back on my feet. There in Boston, I worked three jobs and slowly repaid back everything I owed.

This was the conclusion to one chapter in my life and the beginning of the next. Looking back, I appreciated the hardships and valuable lessons learned, for these experiences have shaped my thinking, priorities, and decision-making process. These attributes would be vital in the next chapter of my life where I would meet the Director of Commerce of Vietnam, who told me that I reminded him of himself. I met many other powerful figures who would open their doors to me to do business with them. I've had many people ask me, "With all the different ventures you have done, what was the best investment you have ever made?" Even now, my answer to that question is still the same, "$1." The best investment I have ever made was that one dollar I spent on the cheeseburger for Steve, which ended up saving my life.

CHAPTER 4

DIAMOND
IN THE ROUGH

By CHIRAG SAGAR

Kindergarten Teacher: *Is there a "Shi-rag" in the room?*

Me: *No, you're saying my name wrong. It's Chirag.*

Kindergarten Teacher: *Is that pronounced Craig?*

Me: *No—it's Chirag.*

Kindergarten Teacher: *I think I'm saying that correctly—Shirag?*

Me: *Ok.*

The day I started kindergarten, my name was--and would forever become--butchered. The way my teacher pronounced my name set a precedent for how my classmates would address me. In my seventh-grade math class, I was called "Cigar," and in my ninth grade Spanish class, I was called "She-Rag." I hated roll call.

This was my first time experiencing adversity. The accumulation of these small moments of pressure and unease accumulated over time to form my thick skin. I developed coping mechanisms to get out of my introverted shell and deal with problems head-on. These small moments are also a big reason why I'm comfortable managing people at three different companies, working sales, and getting involved in media.

Background

As a fifth-generation jeweler, my dad's opportunities dwindled as the family jewelry store in Mumbai became overly populated with his siblings and cousins. Immediately after marriage, my parents migrated to Los Angeles. They wanted the opportunity to live the American Dream--to raise a family while providing their children with a better chance to progress in life.

For a few years after they arrived in the U.S., my father worked with my uncle at a jewelry store, learning the ins and outs of the business. But the reason they came to the U.S. was to create their own business. They launched their own diamond wholesale business shortly after I was born which they still run today.

Born in Glendale, California, I had a unique childhood. I grew up with my Mom, Dad, and younger brother alongside my two older cousins, aunt, and uncle. I'm beyond fortunate to say that I have two mothers, two fathers, and three brothers. We're one big, happy Indian-American family.

(Side note: It boggles my mind that Christopher Columbus' mistake in 1492 still confuses people on whether Native Americans are called Indian Americans. When he sailed across the Pacific, he thought he found another route to India. That's why he called Native Americans, Indians. We know this now. Why has it not been corrected? This 500-year-old mistake is the reason people call me a "red-dot, not a feather" Indian. I digress.)

While more and more Americans are raised in households with divorced parents, I was blessed with four parents. In fact, my parents, aunt, and uncle still live together in the same house that I was raised in. They've battled through all of their differences. My father and uncle were busy building their business and making certain we had food on the table while my mother and aunt raised us. They made it work. Our family showed me how you can fight through trials and tribulations when you have a common goal. Their goal was to take care of the family, provide food and shelter for their four children, and ensure they went to college. And, we did.

My family is very close, but we're all very different. Growing up in a household with six males, there was an overabundance of testosterone. My eldest cousin was the more vocal alpha while his younger brother was the comedian in the family. I was the shy, quiet, and analytical kid and my younger brother was the joker and baby of the family. My uncle is very stubborn but very protective. My aunt is a darling and sweet as can be, and my parents were and are still incredibly open. They were willing to let me grow into the person I wanted and needed to be, even though I'm sure they'd be happier if I were a lawyer, doctor, or computer programmer.

Traditionally, Indian families are very conservative. However, unlike many Indian-American families, my family is very liberal. It was an interesting dichotomy growing up with my close kin of Indian family friends. During my youth, my parents had a small community of several hundred Indians who lived nearby. There were 15 relatively close to my age, all somehow related through marriage.

We all faced a similar identity crisis during our childhoods. Neel and Disha, my two closest friends, would get annoyed explaining our family tree and told everyone we were cousins. We had many inside-jokes that only we understood growing up in an Indian household. Having that comfort gave me solace, although they weren't always around. We all went to the same schools but typically were in different classes.

Growing up with a large, loving Indian family was vastly different from my encounter going to a school where I was the only Indian in my class. Although there were thousands of students in the schools I attended, there were less than 10 Indian students in these schools.

My first discrimination experience occurred within the first month of entering first grade. My classmates were accustomed to seeing TV shows where Indians had thick accents like Apu from the Simpsons. When I first started school, the other kids would look at me with puzzled glances, asking, "Why do you talk normal? Don't your people talk funny?" I think I was too sheltered and young to understand I was stereotyped. I shrugged it off and was eventually accepted.

One of our class assignments was to take human cardboard cutouts our teacher gave us and draw a picture of ourselves with crayons. There were different shades of cardboard color to represent our different races. Out of the 20 students, I was the only brown kid in the room. I searched through the cardboards and noticed none of them matched my skin color. Three of the students saw and called me out, saying that I didn't belong with the rest of the group. It was my first time feeling like an outcast. The name butchering was hard, but this was the first time when I wished I could change my skin color.

With my introverted nature and Indian-cultured upbringing, trying to adapt to American culture and fit in with my classmates confused the hell out of me. It only became worse in high school.

I moved to a new school district and had to make new friends. It took several years to feel comfortable, and by then, making new friends didn't feel right. In retrospect, I think I made friends out of necessity rather than because I had met someone I connected with because of our common interests.

In college, I met other Indian-Americans beyond my family who understood the same jokes and had a similar upbringing as me. My roommates and I loved watching the Los Angeles Lakers, going to football games, playing video games, and working our tails off. It was my first opportunity to meet people who looked like me and understood me. In finding my kin, we all noticed that we shared a fascination for business and entrepreneurship.

My Entrepreneurial Journey

"Entrepreneurship" was a buzzword creeping its way through society as startups and tech companies began to replace Wall Street as the go-to post-college job choice. Inspired by my parent's success in their diamond business, I felt it was only natural for me to head in that direction. I got my first taste of entrepreneurship at the University of Southern California.

My first venture was founding a USC chapter of Moneythink, a financial education nonprofit aimed at mentoring underserved high school students and teaching them about the importance of money and basic financial lessons like savings, credit, loans, scholarships, and investments.

We recruited and trained college students to serve as mentors to the local high school students. It fascinated me how my mentees dealt with their complex problems at home and school, and it was refreshing to see how the program changed some of the student's perspectives on education and life. Moneythink was an inclusion and diversity initiative as much as it was a financial education program.

Once, one of my mentees asked me about my upbringing. I showed him pictures of my family. One of the photos included my family wearing Indian clothing during a Diwali function. He was curious about it, so I talked to him about Indian culture and some of our holidays like Diwali. A few years later, we reconnected, and he informed me that he had an Indian girlfriend in college. He attributes our conversation to sparking his intellectual curiosity in learning more about Indian culture.

As I helped expand Moneythink to other Los Angeles universities, I was curious what I would do post-graduation. One of the things I always wanted to do was travel to China, as I was planning to get a minor in Mandarin. In between my junior and senior year at USC, I went to China to learn about the culture, norms, and business opportunities there--and to test my Mandarin. It became an opportunity to uncover secrets about myself that I wouldn't have learned living at home, in the safety net of Los Angeles.

China

Living in Shaoxing, China allowed me to become comfortable as an introvert with extroverted tendencies. From exploring the city to ordering food and asking for directions, I had to force myself to speak Mandarin and communicate with the locals. It was a basic survival instinct. I became the most fluent I've ever been.

This ability to push myself out of my comfort zone is what has allowed me to make sales in business because as an introvert, I'm constantly in my own head. In China, I was able to place myself in other people's shoes before asking them for help. I analyzed their behavior, mannerisms, timing, clothes, and other variables, all within a fraction of a second, to figure out how I'd approach them to build that immediate connection.

For example, when I was taking a cab to my hotel, the cab driver noticed my Kobe Bryant t-shirt. He spoke to me the entire way to my destination, him practicing his English, while I practiced my Chinese. We kept the conversation mostly focused on basketball, but then I noticed a photo of his family. I asked him about his kids and about his job. The conversation lasted about 20 minutes. He didn't charge me a fee, but I tipped him anyway. We were both happy to make a new friend. Traveling forced me to empathize with people who are different from me and to understand myself through a different lens.

From my first-hand experience, I saw how the Chinese functioned very efficiently in how they operated their hospitals, real estate, community, and ability to process information. By seeing how they viewed the world, it became clear to me the prominent role Asians would play in the world. This is where I learned about the importance of diversity and how it provides different perspectives to view and solve problems. This experience showed me how diversity fosters innovation as it sparked new ideas during my travels and insights about Chinese culture and how Americans could learn from their efficiency.

Fast-forward to today; I work with diverse business partners running a full-service marketing agency called Digital Luxury Agency. I'm also the partner of an online magazine called Destination Luxury and run a book publishing company called Money Matters Top Tips. All of these companies have an inclusive and diverse culture that is inspired by my family, school and university experiences, and travels. I am grateful for the role that diversity and inclusion played in my entrepreneurial journey, including these three initiatives that I'm involved with.

1. Global Shapers: An Initiative of the World Economic Forum

The World Economic Forum cultivates significant world leaders, top executives from Fortune 500 companies, nonprofit leaders, and politicians to Davos to explore solutions to major world-pressing issues. They realized that the future generations didn't have a voice or seat at the table, so they created the Global Shaper Hub community, comprised of 7,000 members from hundreds of global cities. I joined the Chicago Shaper Hub and recently transferred to the Los Angeles hub, where I learned about the impact the collective was making on its local community. Some of these projects include galvanizing Millennials to join Neighborhood Councils and partnering with the City of Los Angeles to work on Hackathons (or Futurethon).

Global Shapers are an intentionally selected diverse group of 20 to 30-year-olds making their mark at a young age, blossoming into future world leaders, with the time to commit to "shaping" their local cities. Each city in the community tries to select individuals that represent every part of their town.

Though volunteers, each hub's mission is to create projects that can impact the city in some way, shape, or form. The hub's goal is to work on a problem that all members of that hub can approach on a united front, leveraging members' various backgrounds, skill sets, and abilities.

If you had a diversity checklist, this group hit all of the marks. It's been interesting traveling to different cities like Hong Kong, Chicago, Los Angeles, Nassau, Miami, and Bangkok to meet Shapers from all around the world. Though we're from different regions, the impact we want to make is similar. We have a platform to participate and inform world-renowned leaders and decision makers who are addressing issues that face young people and future generations.

2. USC's Asian Pacific Alumni Association's Board of Directors

Another opportunity that expanded my understanding of diversity and inclusion was joining USC's Asian Pacific Alumni Association's Board of Directors. Our mission is to raise money for scholarships and re-engage USC Asian alumni that haven't reconnected with their alma mater since graduating. Fortunately, I was the youngest board member when I joined. I learned from my fellow board members about what it's like in the Asian community and how we're underrepresented in leadership positions within the political sector, private sector, nonprofit sector, and within the university.

My fellow board directors are executives of large corporations, making an impact in the political sector, or are successful founders and CEOs of their own companies. They have decision-making power and have influence in their respective communities, industries, and companies.

Every year, we have roughly 30 members spreading awareness about Asian USC students. I'm proud that my alma mater has focused on attracting the best talent and students from around the world. I've recently started to travel to Asia for work more frequently, so I've been focused on creating events to connect with alumni who've lost touch with the USC community in Hong Kong and Mumbai.

USC just became the first university to reach gender parity with more females than males attending their MBA program. USC also has alumni boards focused on Latino and African Americans as well as LGBTQ communities and women-focused groups to attract top talent and raise money for scholarships. Most universities and large corporations now have boards like this that are focused on engaging diverse communities. Diversity sells.

(Thank you to Catherine Park and Jaime Lee for giving me this opportunity to join USC's Asian Pacific Alumni Association Board.)

3. Becoming Founding Chairman of an Advisory Board

I've joined several boards ranging from nonprofits to start-ups and alumni programs at USC. I've also run several different companies. After joining so many boards, I wanted to put into practice what I had learned and create a board. That opportunity arose when the CEO of a globalization conference called GetGlobal asked me to create an advisory board that we felt could be more impactful to the GetGlobal program and the large globalization conferences they host around the world.

Implementing and creating a board was the next evolution in my understanding the role diversity and inclusion could play in making GetGlobal, or any company for that matter, more successful. Tasked with identifying, recruiting, and building a board with several different committees, I built out a 30-member board, containing a range of skill sets and ages, and covering a span of 12 industries and many ethnic backgrounds. It's hard to find people that have decision-making power, but who aren't too busy to volunteer their time and provide impact and value to the program. My most significant insight is that this process cannot be rushed. Board members dropped, and we became smarter with who we approached to find replacements. Experience, passion, and most importantly, time commitment to the cause trump all other traits. Finding people willing to put in the time brought more value than decision-makers who simply lent a name.

Conclusion

From my upbringing, travels abroad, university education, and entrepreneurial journey, the one thing I've learned about diversity is that it opens doors you cannot open yourself. It directly impacts the bottom-line of businesses, creates and builds character, and ultimately shows that we're all human with the same basic needs and desires. Diversity fosters innovation, while inclusion forms the backbone for support. My family was my backbone during times of turmoil. I joke with my parents, aunt and uncle that their offspring are "diamonds in the rough" because our family and society provided the fixated pressure we needed to make us the people we are today.

And, in case you're still wondering: how do you pronounce my name?

Well, I used to live in Chicago, and my friend Andre used to call me "Chirago in Chicago" without the "o" at the end. The "Ch" in my name is pronounced like the word "church." It's Chirag.

CHAPTER 5

A HUNDRED COUNTRIES TO MY FAMILY HOME

By CHRISTINE DRINAN

I was raised in the predominantly white suburbs of Chicago by Filipino immigrant parents and spent most of my early life struggling to fit in with the "American" kids. It wasn't until this past summer that I visited my parent's homeland of the Philippines for the first time. The Philippines was the hundredth country I visited on my journey to join the less than 95 individuals who have visited every country in the world. You see, I travel for a living.

I essentially created my dream job out of the things I love to do: building a business, refining the art of storytelling, and traveling around the world. Along the way, I created a viable, sustainable company that has progressed from the startup phase and is well on its way to scale for that unicorn valuation. I am the founder of

Galavante, a luxury travel media and concierge company. Our mission is to inform, entertain, and inspire you to travel through our online magazine, travel, and lifestyle TV show, and travel concierge.

While I was always entrepreneurial in spirit, I spent most of my career working in finance at the private equity firm Blackstone. I know--it's an uncommon leap from there to becoming an entrepreneur. I'm pretty sure that when I started my company most of my colleagues thought I had suffered a psychotic breakdown, and that I would soon be back in my cubicle doing TPS reports alongside them. Well, it's been eight years this December since I set off on this entrepreneurial adventure and somehow we're still growing every day. I wake up early every morning without an alarm clock, excited to get to work. I love what I do, and I know in many ways that my success is rooted in my background, the adversity and discrimination I faced, and my upbringing as a first generation American.

This is maybe the first time in my life I am acknowledging my heritage, the first time I have felt comfortable writing about the challenges I have faced. Until relatively recently, I did not have a significant connection to my Filipino ancestry. This was partly because my parents did not instill in me a deep understanding of my heritage, as they felt we needed to be raised as Americans to survive. I also just wanted to be a normal kid. Growing up in white suburban Illinois with my ethnicity required me to disconnect from our customs to fit in. It was tough growing up as the daughter of immigrants in my day and age, as racism was even more outwardly prevalent than it is today. As a child, boys on the playground would make fun of me because I was "Chinese" and pull their eyes back and pretend to speak in an Asian language. Their parents didn't care, and I'm sure my parents felt that same prejudice from them.

Growing up in the suburbs of Elmhurst and Wheaton, I was often the only Asian in my class at school, and I was bullied by many of the other children just because of how I looked. When it came time for me to date, my girlfriends often told me that I couldn't date a white boy because "What would our children look like?" I had to find someone of "my kind" to date. (Of course, I've since learned that mixed babies are stunningly beautiful and often become bionic children who are exceptionally good at everything they do). Once in high school, when I had a huge crush on the cutest jock in school, a close girlfriend took me aside to let me know that while he thought I was nice, he couldn't date me because I was Asian. (Note to "my friend": he did date me instead of you. And I broke his heart.)

In high school, there were so many days where I struggled with discrimination. In retrospect, those experiences helped me become the tough-as-nails, emotionally strong individual I am today. I was always at the top of my class. Personally, I learned very early to pay attention to the way people think and act. I developed a strong internal core and sense of self. Also, because I had so few real friends, I learned how to be a great friend, a skill that has taken me very far in life. There is something to be said for having to struggle and not peaking in popularity at an early age.

Today, there is very little, if anything, that can keep me down. And while my relationships improved significantly once I started college, I like to think that the discrimination I faced growing up gave me a special empathy for people, a strong sense of self, and the optimism to never give up. I don't dwell on the negative or the past. I move on and rise to the occasion. I wouldn't change any experience I had growing up because it made me who I am today.

Even with the experience of growing up as a first-generation immigrant, I've always identified as an American, and more specifically as a New Yorker, where I have lived for almost my entire adult life. My parents immigrated to the United States more than 40 years ago, and like so many others, they sought to make a better life for themselves. My mother was a nurse and the eldest of five. Her father was generally absent from their lives, leaving my grandmother (the greatest woman on earth), to look after and provide for them. I can only imagine how hard that must have been for her, but I remember her as a beautiful, extraordinary woman with magnetic energy.

Given the circumstances, she and my mother were the best of friends, compatriots, and partners. My grandmother had a plan: My mother was to get her education and go to the United States to lay the foundation for their family to find a better life. And that's exactly what my mother did. She came to the United States alone--as a young nurse in her twenties with no friends or family, she worked tirelessly, using her modest nursing salary to educate her siblings and bring them, along with her mother, to Chicago.

By the time her family arrived, she was in her 30s (spinster age back then), and yet against all the odds, she met a young man and started a family of her own. She returned to the Philippines only once after she left more than 40 years ago, instead dedicating her life to working as hard as she could so that her family would have a beautiful home, enough food on the table, and receive an education. It wasn't until I saw where my mother grew up that I had a real appreciation for how far she had come.

My father came from a similar background, although his parents had a strong partnership and owned farmland in the province of Bicol, where they educated all 12 of their children. In both of my parents' families, everyone except for distant relatives came to the United States, leaving few roots for either one of them to return to.

My parents are traditional when it comes to a career path, so even after eight years, they are still trying to wrap their heads around why I would ever leave a job in finance to be an entrepreneur. But as they've seen my success grow, or at least the fruits of that success, they are starting to come around.

The one thing they do understand is how much I travel, to countries all over the world. I was surprised that they were not initially supportive of me adding the Philippines to that list. We often argued about it, and my parents would become visibly agitated at the thought of me visiting their home country. From their perspective, the Philippines had become a dangerous place; even with all of my travel experience, they believed it would be too difficult for me to handle myself there. I told them that they had nothing to worry about. I am a savvy world traveler--if I had pursued a different vocation, it could have been war correspondent. I told them I would save the Philippines for my hundredth country, which I assured them was a long way off. It was always my plan to make the Philippines my hundredth country--a milestone for any traveler. Before I knew it, the number 100 crept up, and 2018 became the year to make my voyage.

I'm still not sure how my parents figured it out--I think they spy on my Instagram and were secretly tallying my countries--but my mother called more frequently than normal before my trip to Asia this summer. At first, I didn't return her calls, as I planned to wait until after I returned to tell them about my trip. I just didn't want to argue about it or have them worry about me. But after several calls and incessant messages, I finally had to return her calls. I naively thought that I could avoid the topic, but with her Spidey-sense, my mother outright asked me if I was traveling to the Philippines. I put on my grown-up pants and told my mother the truth: Yes, I was going to the Philippines and I would be leaving in three days. There was a stunned silence, which is rare for a lady like my mother who is seldom at a loss for words.

I had tracked down a long-lost relative (my Uncle Ramon, a cousin of my mother's and the only relative we had left in the Philippines) through his wife, Abigail, on Facebook. We arranged to meet, as I really wanted to see where my mom grew up. It wouldn't be possible to go to my father's hometown, as it was in a less populous province and I had no connections to even his distant relatives.

I was the most curious to see where my grandmother came from, as she raised me until I was 7 years old. My happiest memories of childhood involve my grandmother, and I believe she's still calling in favors for me today up in heaven. In her honor, while I was in Manila, I donated art supplies on behalf of the Christopher Foundation for the Arts. I brought each girl in the orphanage a new shirt and ordered in a special dinner with cupcakes from the very best bakery in the country. I often make donations like this to schools and orphanages when I travel, but this one was extra special because it was for my grandmother.

I walked through the neighborhood of Old Makati and visited my mother's elementary school, where she went to college, and finally the one bedroom apartment she shared with my grandmother and her siblings. I often travel around the world and explore underprivileged neighborhoods, but this one hit home. I looked up at a burnt-out old apartment, abandoned except for a stray cat peering out from a broken window. My grandmother was the foundation of my family, the one with the master plan, but my mother--she was the hustle. Everything they did was the base upon which our family built our lives. My mother and I are not particularly close, but since traveling to her hometown, I've gained a better understanding of her perspective and a deep respect for everything she's achieved.

Indeed, it was because of this visit to the Philippines that I gained a deeper empathy for my parents, and an even greater respect for all they have achieved in life. When I visited them in Chicago after my trip, they were so excited to talk to me about where I had visited and their experiences in the Philippines growing up. They had been following my journey and knew that I stayed at Aman Resorts in the Amanpulo, the most luxurious hotel in the country. My parents never could have afforded to make it to the islands, but they were so excited that I could stay there. Although they were quick to point out it's where celebrities like Beyoncé and Jay-Z stay, even if you took away the entire resort, it is one of the most beautiful beaches I have ever been to in my life.

I like to think of my Amanpulo experience as the moment I realized my family came from one of the most beautiful places on earth. I made new friends who run the hotel, who I know in my heart I will see again. I felt such a strong connection to the people I met on this trip. During lunch one day after my return, I asked my Mom if she would ever consider returning to the Philippines for a visit. She joked and said that she would go only if she could take a "big time" trip like me. Well, Mom, we may just have to make that big time trip happen.

CHAPTER 6

MY CAREER STARTED BY DRIVING A BIG BROWN TRUCK FOR UPS

By **EVA IINO**

I started working for UPS as a part-time clerk while attending college at Cal State Los Angeles majoring in Information Systems. While I was working, I built some spreadsheets on Lotus 123 for the industrial engineering (IE) department at UPS. While they were just simple spreadsheets that had nothing to do with programming, my managers thought they were "out of this world!"

Upon graduating from college, the district industrial engineering manager for UPS offered me a full-time position as an industrial engineering supervisor. (Industrial engineering involves measuring work, efficiencies and time metrics in order to optimize organizational performance.) The catch was, I had to learn the job from the ground up by driving one of those big brown UPS trucks, making deliveries and picking up packages. Because I was going to be in charge of measuring the work, I had to understand the job from an employee's perspective. I also had to "make it" as a driver. In other words, I had to meet or beat the standards set up for the route before I could be promoted. The minimum amount of time I would be out on road would be three months!

I was the very first female Asian American to be offered this opportunity, as I was hired "from the outside instead of promoted from within". I knew I couldn't fail because there were other women at UPS who wanted to move into management positions they were looking to me to set the standard. As you might imagine, at the time, UPS, being a trucking and transportation company, was a male-dominated business. There weren't many women in management, let alone Asian American women.

The other reason I couldn't fail was because my district IE manager told me that if I didn't cut it as a truck driver, I was not going to be able to come back to his team as a clerk. I was 5'4" weighing in at 110 pounds, so the simple task of delivering and picking up packages that weighed up to 70 pounds each was definitely going to be a challenge for me. The brown UPS uniform wasn't even stocked in my size; it had to be special-ordered.

I got trained like any other UPS truck driver with three days with a supervisor who would walk me through the proper methods of how to drive safely and how to pick up and deliver packages. The fourth day, I drove and performed the work while the supervisor rode with me. From the fifth day on, I was on my own. For those big heavy packages, I had to use my whole body weight to pick up and move the packages. To make up time, I learned to take shorter than prescribed breaks and pick up the pace at stops. By the end of my second week, I was able to meet the standards and was even able to come in before my prescribed time. Customers were shocked at first to see me climb out of the big brown UPS truck. Most were nice and would help me when I came to pick up packages. There were always a few people (jerks) who wanted to see me work. They wanted to see if I could lift those 70 pounds. I showed them I could but I also lost 10 pounds and was bruised from my neck down due to all the heavy lifting and loading.

Three months to the day after I started driving that truck, my district IE manager found me on my route and surprised me while I was on road. He stopped me while I was approaching one of my stops to tell me that as of the next day, I would be promoted to be his industrial engineering supervisor! I was almost 22 years old. Now, the three months I drove that truck route was almost 34 years ago.

So I began working for a department where I was the only female. Every training session, every meeting, I was surrounded by men. I knew I had to be more than prepared at meetings and never opened my mouth unless I had all my facts straight. I worked 12 to 14 hour days to prove that I belonged there. I took every assignment I was given including a six-month assignment in Greenwich, Connecticut (the corporate headquarters for UPS at that time). I knew I was being tested to see how much "brown blood" I had in me. I commuted from Los Angeles to New York every week to work on this project. Frequently, I would have to stay in Connecticut for two weeks before returning home. This definitely took a toll on my personal relationship with my fiancée at the time.

Since I was new to management, I picked out a mentor, someone I wanted to model my management style after. This happened to be my district IE manager, a white man who had a reputation for being tough and mean. Luckily, I was never on the receiving end of his tirades. In fact, he was the one who moved me from operation to operation to insure that I was well versed in all aspects of our business. Within four years, I was promoted to an IE manager, the first Asian American female to ever rise to that level. I owe a lot to my former manager and still feel indebted to him for lighting my path.

Once I had been promoted to manager, I was able to shape and develop my own team of IE supervisors. I added color to my team by hiring more females and minorities not because of their gender or race but because they were the most qualified. These were all "outside hires" which meant they had to drive a truck, just like I had. They all did and they all made it. I was able to build a great team; we worked well together and were always well respected in the region. Whenever I had staff meetings, we'd start off with a game to illustrate a leadership skill. I was focused on training my people to prepare them for their next steps. I learned that a great leader always develops their people so that they may one day take your place.

I also learned that even though I was the only woman in management (my counterparts in other districts were all male), I didn't have to act or try to be like a man to fit in. I needed to build relationships supporting other departments within the company. To work smoothly together, we also had to earn their confidence. Although I used my gender to my advantage, as a woman in a male dominated company, I could use my female "charm" to build relationships, I never backed down from confrontation or let anyone walk all over me.

My philosophy for success as a leader placed high importance on trust. I wanted my team to know that I was always going to be there for them and that I would take the fall for any mishaps or mistakes they may make. I had their backs. This allowed them to try new things and not be afraid that they might fail. My only caveat was that they needed to inform me of any mishaps so that I could be prepared for the consequences.

Nine years after driving that big brown truck, I was called in to my district IE manager's office where he informed me that I was ready to become his equal. A district manager! Again, I would be the first Asian female to hold this position at UPS. I knew the unwritten rules: I would have to relocate to a city that was not my choice. If I didn't accept this, my career would be over and I would not be considered for any other promotions. I struggled with this decision, as I had worked so hard to get to this point in my career. At that time, I was engaged to a man who had a thriving career of his own as a stockbroker. To accept the promotion, I would have had to ask him to move and start over. As an Asian woman, I thought that I could not do that to him, he is the man and I am secondary as his fiancée. I ended up turning down that promotion knowing that my career would be at a standstill. This was one of the toughest choices I ever had to make.

But, I have a guardian angel as I have always been blessed. My mother passed away when I was 12 years old, leaving me to care for and parent my three younger brothers as well as my Dad. I always believed that my mother watched out for me. It was my way of dealing with her loss.

I received a phone call shortly after I turned down my promotion. It was from the Pacific Regional IE Manager, my boss' boss. He offered me a position working for him as his region IE manager. He told me that sometimes, you just have to do the right thing and for him, the right thing was to pick me up and bring me on his team. I was shocked and humbled. I accepted the position and vowed to never disappoint him. My area of responsibility would be all of Southern California south of San Luis Obispo and states of Arizona & Utah.

Incidentally, I also decided to call off my wedding not all because of the demands of my career; there were many other personal issues that led to this decision. But I was free to travel frequently and enjoyed my job. But I was no longer a young woman: I was going to be 32 and if I wanted a family life, I needed to make a change.

Soon enough, an opportunity arose. UPS offered a buyout to all managers to in order to downsize their management structure. Management was compensated with stock and UPS was not public at that time. I had never thought about leaving UPS until one of my supervisors on my team (a woman I had hired) told me to think about it seriously, she was going to take the deal. After much contemplation on the very last day, on the very last hour, I submitted my paperwork. Leave the company I poured my heart and soul into?

What was I getting myself into?

But it was an opportunity. I now was free to pursue a new beginning, I didn't know what that beginning would look like but knew that it had to be more balanced so that I could juggle a career and a personal life. That was 23 years ago.

Fast forward to present day. I met and married a wonderful man, the love of my life, my soulmate and best friend. We have 13 year old twins (a boy and a girl) and have everything I could ever ask for.

After leaving UPS another large male dominated transportation company wanted to meet with me. Because their work culture seemed different, I was talked into joining the company. I was promoted a couple times and after about 15 years, I was offered a position as a managing director.

I turned it down. To this day, I am fine with not accepting the position. My priority was and continues to be our family. It was important for me to be available for my children and my family: to attend recitals, performances and sports events that the twins are part of. This time around, I am older and certainly wiser. I don't need a title to validate my abilities and define who I am.

I love the company I work for. Because they put their people first, I was not penalized for turning down the promotion. I have a great boss. When I first started with the company, I picked another white male as my mentor. It was he who offered me a flexible schedule when I was trying to get pregnant. It was he who saw that I could be trusted to not have to go into an office every day to get my work done, something that was never offered before in my department. He was the one who allowed me to achieve balance between my career and my other responsibilities of being a mom and wife. Because he was so generous with me, I worked to ensure that I would never let him down.

I currently hold a regional position that encompasses everything west of Denver. My white male mentor who first offered me my flexible schedule? He's now the Number One person who reports directly to the President and CEO. I can only smile when I think about him and all that he's accomplished. To this day, he still looks out for me.

I have seen a slow change during these last 34 years in the transportation industry. More and more women are being promoted into top positions. It could be because I now work for a more progressive company, but I hope that this is the trend across the industry. I am grateful for my beginnings. Driving a big brown UPS truck taught me grit, perseverance, and not to let anyone walk all over me. I had to prove to my white male counterparts that I could do the job and that I earned my right to my seat at the table. I know that I am no different than they are, because I took the same path they did to become promoted and recognized in my career.

Building trusting relationships with your peers and those you support is essential. I believe that being a woman can work to your advantage, learn how to use it to your benefit. Whether it's navigating relationships, analyzing issues or developing solutions, sometimes it helps to be a woman.

It is my goal to continue to educate my peers and to help them not judge people by what you see, on the surface. When my husband and I were choosing names for our daughter 13 years ago, I was adamant that we not choose a name that would give away her gender on paper. I didn't want her to have a disadvantage right from the start. We continue to teach our children to be the best that they can be, to always do what's right and that doors will open for them. After all, they too have a guardian angel!

CHAPTER 7

BREAKING DOWN BARRIERS IN INTERIOR DESIGN AND CONSTRUCTION

By **HANNA LI**

"You can't sit at that table, Hanna," my mother said as I picked up my chopsticks ready to eat. I had sneaked up to the "adults table," filled with the men in my family who would talk about subjects I found fascinating. Did it matter that my family regarded it as the men's table? To me, it was not even a consideration. The patriarchs discussed topics and analyzed matters that deeply challenged my young imagination. However, I was supposed to sit at the women's table, where conversations focused on motherhood and preadolescent education. Though I recognize the value of these conversations, I've always been more interested in business and entrepreneurship. Throughout my life, I've challenged biases such as race, gender, and age as I worked to break the invisible chains I was bound by in the form of gender-normative pressures from my family. Breaking down barriers wasn't what I set out to do, but it's what I had to do.

I grew up in a large family of woodworkers, builders, and mechanics. I never fit the mold of the "trophy wife" I was raised to become. Watching my father work was the first experience that piqued my interest in building things with my hands. Once I started making things, that initial curiosity turned into an intense passion that took on a life force of its own. I had awakened my inner love for design and crafting and it wasn't something I could simply push back into the closet. My mother used to say, "give her crayons and paper, and she'll be lost in her world all day." What's more, my path to be an artist was even "seen upon" by the most influential fortune reader in my village who foretold I carried a bloodline for the creative field.

I grew up in a traditional patriarchal household, where my parents' goals were for me to become a good wife, look after a man, and raise children of my own. This was the tradition in my culture. Of course, as an artist, I went against the grain.

When I moved to the United States for school, everything opened for me. I was taught I could be whatever I wanted to be. There was a completely different support system and view of what a woman could accomplish. But now, I had another challenge to overcome: I was the only immigrant in my grade who had to learn my ABCs from scratch. I was naturally shy, so I often excluded myself from social events in fear of being judged. Many days, I would eat in the art studio alone so I could avoid the lunch crowds. When I was alone, it took much less effort just to be myself. Thus, instead of a busy social calendar, I found solace in my work and in my art. I could be carried away working on a canvas for hours without a break. What was in between the strokes, the layering opacity of colors, the blurring of space and dimensions--all had power and meaning to me. Fueling my creativity was important to me; I didn't care about the rest of high school social gossip.

"You can't be in here, it's for Mathletes only," a group of girls once told me--more voices telling me what I couldn't do. Little did they know, I was taking Advanced Placement Statistics. I did belong in that class. I figured they thought that because I was an art-geek and had trouble with English, my capacity for learning was somehow inferior to theirs. Many times, false judgments are made based on the way a person looks or sounds. My high school experience taught me to never jump to conclusions before truly getting to know someone.

And all my hard work was about to pay off. During my senior year in high school, The Rhode Island School of Design accepted me into their furniture design program, making me only the second person in 30 years to be accepted in this program from my school. Although I was thrilled, my grandfather would make jokes about "how we sent our children all the way to America to pursue a better life, to grow up as lawyers, developers, and doctors, yet she turned out to be a woodworker. Just like one of us!" It's funny--the apple indeed didn't fall far from the tree. Of course, it was a big surprise to my family that I would take up what they consider a "man's job." As you can imagine, woodworking was a very male-dominated world.

In college at RISD, I was made fun of for wearing heels to class, as 90 percent of the boys wore Timberland boots and flannel button-down shirts. Just because I have to perform heavy-duty millwork doesn't mean I can't look fabulous doing it! I also encountered the physical struggles of being a petite woman in a masculine environment. Woodworking shops are loud and intense. My shoulders still have micro-tears on them from the many days of carrying heavy wooden planks. The program was competitive, but I didn't waver. I struggled, but ambition runs in my blood. Not only was I able to successfully finish the program, I was also awarded my own space in the RISD museum to present my final exhibition, a display of aluminum chandeliers in the shape of manta rays that I called "Manta Flight."

While at RISD, I also pursued a minor in environmental science from Brown University. Going to school with some of the most brilliant people in the country often made me feel alienated and intimidated. I wondered: Did I really stack up to these Ivy Leaguers? It felt like I wasn't good enough to compete. It was only after graduating that I appreciated what an amazing experience it was. We often worked in the shop for three days straight. All my classmates at RISD slept in the shop at one time or another. If it was two in the morning and you were not in the shop, you were slacking. We were trained through this experience to have excellence engrained into the fiber of our being. All-nighters and meeting impossible deadlines was just a part of the culture that engulfed us all. My classmates have gone off to make the world a better place. They still inspire me to be the best I can be.

Connecting to design was difficult for me in the college. Fine arts came naturally, but design was different. Developing my sense of identity in product design took some re-wiring. Who was I as a designer? Even in woodworking, the concepts were manual and meticulous. For example, American traditions were different from the Chinese joinery I was accustomed too. The work was a constant reminder of how different I was. I didn't cross the bridge of self-realization as a designer in my college days. But I think this feeling of being lost is what caused me to push myself so hard after college to find my own style.

Post college, after training for a few months as a design assistant, I founded my own design firm. Due to the influx of foreign wealth in Los Angeles, my first few clients were rich Chinese entrepreneurs from overseas. Here I was, a fresh graduate tasked with client relations. I did everything from putting together business proposals and going on-site to supervising the final interior installs. Why would a new graduate want all this responsibility? Being Chinese was finally paying off for me. I spoke a dialect called Teo Chew that was native to my village. I also spoke Mandarin and Cantonese because my family is from the Guangdong region. Being well versed in three languages gave me an immense leg up on other local firms. I sat in on every business deal that involved Chinese clients.

Young, inexperienced, and eager, I wanted to develop my own style. My first boss thought I was crazy to leave her and go into business for myself. She told me, "You won't have enough experience even after 10 years." Naturally, my lack of experience didn't bother me. I understood exactly what our overseas clients wanted. My vision was to merge what I was trained to do and what I saw from a Chinoiserie style (Asian-French style) with Spanish contemporary design, which was wildly popular in Los Angeles in the mid 2000s. My perceived weakness became my greatest strength. I no longer had to be afraid to be Chinese American. I could develop a style that was consistent with who I was. An added bonus was that I could also communicate with the clients and factories overseas that had difficulty engaging with designers who didn't speak their native tongue. Being able to cultivate these relationships allowed me to flourish in areas that other local firms couldn't.

From that point on, my career advanced quickly. Word had gotten out about the quality of my work and design. As my business expanded and referrals mounted, I shifted towards a design-and-build model. My aim was to create a full-service design firm committed to doing build-outs, remodels, additions, interior finishes, and interior design. It felt like I was back in shop class all over again, with men in boots cutting lumber and saws blaring. I loved it. This time around, I felt like I was in control. I didn't have random assignments or expectations to deal with. Instead, I was working to fulfill the fantasies of my clients and to bring their stories to life. Of course, everything wasn't all sunshine and roses.

This field is extremely competitive. It can often feel like you are going on a casting call when bidding on a job, with a lobby full of people waiting for their turn to meet with the client. Everyone wants the project, but only one will win. For example, I was recently bidding on a job for former professional boxer Oscar de la Hoya. I was competing with seven other firms for the assignment and I was the youngest person in the room by a long stretch. This brought up some of the same doubts I'd had in the past. Am I too young? Will the client think because I am Asian American, my designs will be too disconnected for his taste? Will the client prefer to work with a male? These little doubts have a way of persisting despite success. But they are not always based on reality. After several meetings, to my absolute surprise, we won the Oscar de la Hoya bid and my work is now scheduled to be featured in a prestigious national magazine, making me the youngest designer featured in the luxury celebrity category.

So, what next? I see an opportunity to build a streamlined and well-organized construction and design company. The current model of how design and construction companies function is somewhat backward. The contractor relies on subcontractors from many different trades to finish a job. Subcontractors are not always reliable. If someone doesn't show up, the job doesn't get done. The good news is that if I am facing these challenges, so is my competition. But I realized that if these services didn't stand independent of one another and instead were cohesive, the client would get the best product in the shortest amount of time. I am in the process of getting my contractor's license to see if I can tackle this problem and create an even better experience for my current and future clients.

For the women considering entering the male-dominated fields of construction and design, I want to tell you there is hope. Although to date, there have only been a couple women to win the Pritzker Architecture Prize (architecture's Nobel Prize), I encourage women who want to pick up a hammer to do it. Don't be discouraged and decide that it's a "man's job." Fix your own leaky faucet if you want to. Women are naturally more detail-oriented and sensitive to different design elements, and we truly have the power to build the houses of tomorrow. I look forward to creating a better-designed future for everyone.

CHAPTER 8

THE ABC'S OF INCLUSION:
Acceptance, Belonging, Compassion

By **JAPMAN BAJAJ**

"Yeah. It's a knife. What are you going to do about it?"

As an 11-year-old kid with no friends and the frequent target of bullies, these aren't words you want to hear. Especially when they're being said by three of the more aggressive bullies and older kids at your school.

This was just another day at school for me. I was reminded early and often that I was too different to be normal, which sometimes resulted in visible scars, other times invisible ones.

This story will have a happy ending. I'm trying to make sure of it.

It's important to share where my story begins. I am a Canadian-born Sikh, which made parts of my upbringing difficult. I had to learn how to confront and establish an individual identity and, as I grew older, I had to learn acceptance and inclusion. Today, my story is one of championing diversity. I must warn you in advance: These early stories may be uncomfortable to hear, as they are uncomfortable to share. I hope this shared vulnerability and discomfort creates connection, fosters dialogue, and impacts us for the better.

Generally speaking, we like to think of childhood as an innocent time full of discovery and wonder, curiosity and dreaming. While my childhood certainly had these components, it also had the unwanted presence of discrimination. I was bullied extensively as a kid. At the age of 7, I was swarmed by a group of ten other students, held down, and buried in a snow grave on the school playground. None of the students faced consequences even after a teacher intervened. A year later, in math class, a student seated behind me took scissors and cut strands of my hair, despite knowing that uncut hair was a religious obligation that I took seriously.

It didn't matter that I was athletic, loved the local sports team, and watched the same TV shows as my peers. I was regularly shunned at school and insulted based on my appearance. I was once confronted with a knife in a hallway during recess. By sixth grade, I often stayed inside for recess, a short reprieve from the schoolyard bullying. Most teachers were sympathetic and gave me respect, but few intervened or stood up for me directly.

When I got into my first discrimination-related fight in second grade, earning me a detention, I got ice cream from my parents later that night. As immigrants to Canada in the early 1970s, they knew that this country full of gifts and opportunity wasn't going to be roses and rainbows for everyone. They understood that sometimes you must fight simply to be treated like a human being. Picking that fight in second grade did not stop the bullies. Standing up for yourself becomes the status quo. You come to realize that the discrimination doesn't actually go away, it just becomes addressable, and it becomes addressable on a regular basis. Like any good skill, you develop a skill set of dealing with bullies; but the bullies don't stop coming.

On Identity

"My potential is more than can be expressed within the bounds of my race or ethnic identity."
—Arthur Ashe

I grew up in a modest home in suburban Ottawa, Canada, in a predominantly French-Canadian neighborhood. As a turban-wearing Sikh, childhood was difficult. There were many school days that ended with me coming home to my family in tears, seeking solace. The bullying stopped once I got home, and it was replaced by unconditional love and support. My older sisters showered me with love, and my parents and grandmother would strengthen my resolve with compassion and inspiring stories from my heritage. Without them, the ordeals would have been so much worse.

The bullying was consistent until seventh grade. By then, I made some minor changes to be more "mainstream." Still, I questioned why people couldn't accept me just the way I was. My parents and sisters gave me the strength to believe in my own identity, which meant it was incumbent upon the outside world to accept me for who I was. The only problem was that the outside world generally refused to comply.

Although I was born in Ottawa, I was fluent in my native language of Punjabi until the age of 5. When I began school, English became and has remained my dominant language. My name, Japman, was rarely pronounced accurately, and when I taught people how to say my name or other Punjabi words, they were often mocked, teased, or ridiculed; at best, my name was mispronounced. For a brief period, I allowed people to call me JP, a more common name for my French-Canadian neighborhood. The incentive to identify with my mother tongue diminished, and I accepted the anglicized version of my name.

This may seem like the smallest of compromises, but it is one of the many we make in order to achieve a basic human need--a sense of belonging. In August 2018, a new father published a letter to his newborn daughter in Maclean's, a Canadian news magazine, about his very long Sudanese name, and the challenges and gifts it will provide. "You don't know it yet," Elamin Abdelmahmoud writes, "but every time someone asks 'can you spell that?' you're going to feel the sting of lineage, the gentle hand of ancestry." And so, consciously or unconsciously, we compromise the lineage and ancestry we inherited to remove the sting that comes with a complicated ethnic name. Our names are vehicles of our rich heritage and provide a strong sense of intangible belonging through the stories of those that came before us. It may not seem like a big ask, but the implications can be significant.

On Inclusion

"When everyone is included, everyone wins"
—Jesse Jackson

Just before I entered university, I was in a serious high-speed car accident that could have been much worse if not for a convergence of coincidences and circumstance. Thankfully, both my passenger and I walked away from the wreck relatively unscathed. In the weeks of recovery that followed, I had the opportunity to spend time with my family, who had travelled to be with me and support my recovery. During this time, I had a profound conversation with a family member who asked me if my near-death experience spurred any insights or lessons that may help guide the rest of my life.

There has been an unending stream of love and support in my life, especially from my sisters and parents, which has been all the more valuable when juxtaposed against the challenges and obstacles that have been placed before me. Throughout my life, I have experienced the pangs of sadness at being overlooked or discounted, the flashes of anger at being ignored, and the sparks of aggression that would lead me to challenge my detractors. And while stories of rebellion and courage in the face of adversity are romanticized in our culture, it would be far better if such stories were relegated to fiction. For so long, my turban and even my skin color served as social barriers which I had no choice but to fight through on a regular basis. Adversity undoubtedly builds character, but no one should have their basic worth defined by their physical identity.

Back to the conversation with my family member, I replied "One thing I'd like to do is give everyone a chance. I'd like to give everyone I meet and with whom I interact the opportunity to teach me something. I'd like to be able to see the value that every individual brings to the table."

As a senior in university, I uncovered my passion for entrepreneurship. Suddenly everything was different. My school's entrepreneurship club had a shortage of executives, and as someone who had long exhibited leadership behaviors, I decided to put my name forward. What I originally thought would be a small commitment quickly turned into some of the most memorable experiences and friendships of my life. For the first time in my life, it felt like I was tapping into my full potential, and creating impact in an exponential way. I entered a space where my efforts were more meaningful than any other external factor. Although there were still some biases, the entrepreneurial ecosystems were used to different types of people with different backgrounds creating meaningful impact. The entrepreneurial journey showed me a utopian world based on individual contributions over appearance. I was accepted first and foremost because I was an entrepreneur, and judged based on my intelligence, abilities, and impact. For the first time in my life, I was part of a community that was built on acceptance--all you had to do was bring yourself and your talents and contribute something.

Entrepreneurship depends on the balanced tension between education, skills, and connections and contexts, perspectives, and biases. Entrepreneurship welcomes creativity and passion as equals with education and contacts, and we continue to learn about the value of diversity in entrepreneurship. Corporate cultures are catching up, albeit very slowly. We're not yet at a place where diversity is measured on a financial statement, but perhaps we're getting close.

Championing Diversity

"Innovation is all about people. Innovation thrives when the population is diverse, accepting, and willing to cooperate."
—Vivek Wadhwa

Over the past 10 years, my career has taken me from summer student with the government of Canada to co-founder and CFO of a technology company to executive at a major global telecommunications firm. One of the most valuable factors behind my early success has been mentorship, both received and offered.

Mentorship has served as an incredible learning platform, enabling me to be the person I aspired to be after my car accident. It connected me with hundreds of aspiring entrepreneurs, immigrant youth from many different backgrounds, and young adults battling with their own identities, ethnicities, orientations, and challenges. In 2009, mentorship inspired me to create a city-wide networking organization for young millennials in Ottawa, connecting high-achieving new professionals. The following year, I had the benefit of a number of expert mentors who guided me through the challenges and rollercoasters of entrepreneurship as I launched my first start-up. Mentoring entrepreneurs gives me an opportunity to learn what is happening at the cutting edge of a variety of fields, keeping me relevant in an ever-changing world as well as giving back to the community. It eased my transition into a new city, and it continues to inform my rise as a business, community, and political leader in Canada.

As a Canadian, I live in a country that proudly and openly celebrates diversity, and our most prominent politicians point to diversity as our nation's greatest strength. We welcome refugees and immigrants from around the world, and we celebrate our multiculturalism in ways that allow people to maintain their heritage while still integrating into society.

Over the past decade, I have engaged in countless initiatives to help tell the story of Canadian Sikhs. I've learned that many Canadians are quiet but inquisitive, concerned with disrespecting me with their "possibly offensive" questions more than with satisfying their intellectual thirst. There's something tragic yet beautiful about the fact that the people I want to approach me often don't out of a fear of offending. When they do, they build bridges, empathize, and develop a better understanding about their neighbor. They can't be offensive because their intent is innocent, positive, and loving. They begin their question with, "I'm really sorry if this is an offensive question, but I was wondering..." They innocently and respectfully aim to learn more about something they don't understand.

Despite Canada's commendable commitment to diversity, even Canada doesn't always get it right. In 2012, the province of Quebec upheld the decision of the Quebec Soccer Federation to prohibit soccer players from wearing religious head coverings. While it mirrored the rules of soccer's international governing body, FIFA eliminated the rule in 2012, while the Quebec Soccer Federation made no such effort until the end of 2013.

Under the guise of safety--according to the Quebec Soccer Federation, a thin hijab could cause grave injury to a fellow player!-

-children as young as six years old were removed from fields and from their teams due to noncompliance with the rule. Referees were banned from wearing their religious symbols and articles of faith, and turban-wearing and hijab-wearing soccer lovers were deprived of the sport they loved to play.

At the time, I sat on the board of an international human rights organization. We were, on one hand, dismayed by the sheer lack of acceptance and tolerance by a provincial body for "the world's game," even after the international body had relaxed its requirements. On the other hand, we witnessed great acts of leadership, compassion, and unity from multiple communities, as people across color, creed, and faith banded together to lobby against the rule. Ultimately, the Federation had no choice but to respond to public pressure, and all children were once again permitted to play their favorite sport.

These realities challenge our societies even today, and they tend to attack our most innocent and vulnerable. It is--and always will be--the togetherness of communities that allows us to correct social injustices systemically ingrained in our societies. That is when diversity and inclusion thrives--when we bring groups of people together around shared interests, shared goals, shared objectives, and shared visions, we achieve things that we otherwise could not on our own.

Summary
While many people suffer from an identity crisis as they battle with discrimination and exclusivity, I had a different type of crisis. Mine was not a crisis of identity--mine was a crisis of acceptance. What was it that prevented people from looking past the turban on

my head and the color of my skin? What social pressures compelled individuals to behave with maliciousness or apathy toward another person? Why didn't it matter that I was funny, good at sports, intelligent, and compassionate?

Humans need to feel belonging. It is unquestionably sad that some children grow up without the feeling of belonging. Coping with that void is time and energy wasted. It is time and energy diverted from academics, athletics, playing, wondering, imagining, and daydreaming. We have to free up people's willpower and emotional capacity to focus on the things that make them come alive. We achieve belonging by fostering meaningful and genuine connection between people. We don't achieve this sense of belonging by having a requisite number of friends from ethnicities other than our own.

While belonging comes from an internal dialogue between an individual and their surroundings, diversity and inclusion attempts to measure and evaluate the ability of an environment to cultivate belonging. Diversity and inclusion are more than quotas and checkboxes. They are far more nuanced, going beyond visible characteristics.

Throughout this book you will read stories of amazing and talented men and women confronting their identities and their sense of place. But even among each of us, our contexts are different. And yet, it is naturally easier to measure and manage diversity in workplaces and corporate environments through a person's appearance. While a young white boy from my childhood knows little about my cultural and ethnic contexts, a young Sikh boy in Fresno, California, or Brampton, Ontario--cities with a large population of Sikhs--may also not relate to my life journey. It is as imperative as ever to champion diversity now: to ask better questions about what diversity really is, and what diversity really means.

On one hand, it requires us to have our eyes wide open and to take the steps to understand contexts, realities, and implicit biases that may be unconsciously hampering our ability to be inclusive. It requires us to get uncomfortable with stories we may not want to confront about our neighbors, stories that are stunning in their cruelty, stories that we don't relate to despite sharing a street. On the other hand, it is the journey to blindness, in which the way a person looks and moves plays no role in the way you evaluate them. It is a commitment to value a person as they are, including their stories, their histories, their pains, and their brains.

Identity is so much more than the way we look. It is deeply intersectional. I'm not just a Sikh. I'm a Canadian. I'm a man, a brother, an uncle. I'm an entrepreneur. I'm a corporate executive. Dozens of other things ultimately make me who I am. But I'm not unique--I am absolutely certain that there is something about me that any other person on earth could relate to.

I challenge you to find that relatability with everyone in your life. I challenge you to work harder to identify commonality with people that are different from you. I challenge you to offer mentorship and opportunity to those over whom you have any degree of privilege. I challenge you to be an active ally to those who need allies.

Let's all make sure even more stories have a happy ending.

CHAPTER 9

IT'S IN THE NUMBERS

By JENEVIERE KIM

She jumps out of a helicopter and starts falling. With only 12 seconds left on the clock, she takes apart the bomb from the man's vest in the sky. As the bomb goes off in mid-air, doing no harm to anyone, the man starts spiraling down to the ground. She gets a hold of him and tightens her grip then releases her parachute and lands safely on a moving boat saving his life and hers. She takes off her helmet, and with the wind flowing through her long, black hair she reveals herself to be Alex Munday: a character portrayed by Lucy Liu in Charlie's Angels 2000 release.

At that moment, I realized that it was possible for me to become an actress. As a little girl, I was in complete awe to see an Asian woman be such a "bad chick," as one might say, on the big screen. I had thought that you had to be a tall, blonde model to pursue an acting career. When I saw Lucy Liu, someone who looked like me, as one of the leads in a Hollywood movie--equal to her co-stars Drew Barrymore and Cameron Diaz--it gave me the inspiration I needed.

I knew as a kid that I wanted to be some sort of entertainer. I would stand on top of my bed and sing, acting like I was performing to an audience. I reenacted scenes that I had seen on television (I still do this). I would even create dramas for my barbies, spending hours having them go through journeys of turmoil, sadness, and even death. I knew how to be dramatic. My parents saw this, but it didn't once cross their minds to put me in some sort of art school.

I have traditional Asian parents that didn't understand the concept of making a living as an artist. They had high hopes for me to have a secure, high paying job (In part so I could financially take care of them.) Yet, they failed to see how encouragement would yield the highest payoff. Instead of saying, "you can do it" or "I believe in you," they were constantly telling me how I wasn't good enough. As I grew up, one of the challenges I had to overcome was shaking off that negativity. They were coming from a place of love, which also held fear: The fear that any parent would have in wanting their children to be well off in life. They loved me the best way they knew how.

I was born in Honolulu, Hawaii, and lived there until elementary school. I was fortunate to not feel like an outcast due to my race because Hawaii has a large population of Asians. Two of my best friends in elementary school were Asian. In fact, the majority of my classmates were Asian. That all changed when we moved to Texas when I was 9 years old. The school system forced me to take English as a Second Language without testing my English abilities. They didn't care that I was more fluent in English than I was in Korean. It wasn't so much that the other students treated me differently because I was an unfamiliar face; it was more that they had a complete lack of knowledge or understanding of my culture.

I grew up in a very chaotic home. My dad wasn't always the nicest to my mom and just a couple of months after we moved, my parents divorced. My mom moved to Korea, so I didn't get to see her. I was in a new place with no friends and no mom. It was a difficult time in my life. When I asked my dad if I could go to acting school, he immediately said, "no." He was a single parent raising my sister and me. He worked all the time. When and who was going to take me to acting classes? It wasn't until after high school, when I worked different jobs to be able to afford acting classes, that I was able to pursue my dream.

I started acting classes at the same time I went to college to receive an economics degree. I wanted to make the parents somewhat happy. I had a full-time job, was a full-time student taking 15 to 18 credits per semester, and acted on top of that. During that time, I felt torn between school and acting. There were times I had to cease acting classes because 15-page thesis papers took way too much time. Yet, when an audition came up in the middle of class, I would leave.

After college, I lived in Dallas and really focused on acting. There were not as many opportunities for leads or main character roles for Asian-Americans in the TV and film industry in Dallas as there would be in Los Angeles or New York. It's tough being in the entertainment industry, but it's even tougher to be a minority, even more so for Asians. According to Data USA, only 5 to 6 percent of working actors from 2014-2016 were Asian, including all roles and not just leads. I've been on the verge of quitting; yet every time, I've been pulled back into it with something telling me not to stop. I believe that something is love. So, I packed up my four-door sedan and moved to Los Angeles.

When I moved, some of my Caucasian friends told me how good it is to be ethnic right now in the industry. I agreed, which then they proceeded to say it's hard being white right now as the industry is diversifying itself. While it's true and exciting that more roles are coming up for minorities, Caucasians by far still receive a majority of the parts. There are more Caucasian actors, but there are still way more roles going to Caucasians. There may not be as many Asian actors, but there aren't as many opportunities for them either. According to the USC School of Communication and Journalism, "of the top 100 films in 2015, 49 films included no speaking or named Asian or Asian-American characters."

One way to start changing this is to make others aware that we don't just fill in a quota. I did an indie film where the executive producer was a woman who was also the co-writer and co-director. We need more women in all roles in Hollywood, and according to the Center for the Study of Women in Television & Film, only 13 percent of directors are female in the top 700 films of 2014. The executive producer of the indie said, "If you add ethnic people then more people will watch your film. If you have an Asian in the film then Asians will watch it. If you have a black person in the film then African-Americans will watch it." I understood what she was saying and there's some truth to it, but my role in this film was a pharmacist. There was nothing in depth about my character. The main actor comes into a pharmacy and buys some medication. I didn't believe that just because she cast me as a pharmacist, more Asians were going to flock on over to the see the film.

Asians are capable of so much more. It's about having the opportunity to do it. From 2007 to 2015, Asians represented less than four percent of characters, but Asian leads can pull in huge successes. Crazy Rich Asians took the top box office for multiple weekends in a row, becoming the most successful studio romantic comedy in nine years. Slumdog Millionaire won eight out of the 10 Academy Awards it was nominated for. We too are the leads. We can act in the roles that an Asian wasn't considered for. We want more diversity and inclusion to start breaking down those barriers. You can also take charge by creating your own material. Create projects of your own and share that with the world. I recently finished a 110-page script, and it's been one of the most rewarding and accomplished feelings I've had.

Although I have a love/hate relationship with L.A., I really do love living here. There's something great about being packed in a city with so many creative people. There's this energetic high. Hollywood is a beast: It can chew you up and spit you back out. I'm fortunate that I have friends and role models who consistently push me to be the best I can be, who remind me to always have great determination and a winning mentality.

I fall in love with acting over and over again. I'm grateful to be a working actress. I write my own scripts and make films with my friends. I support my friend's projects from film to theatre. I recently joined the University of Southern California's film festival committee. It brings me joy to encourage filmmakers to create more content and have their voice be heard. This is also why working with charities have been a dream of mine to give back to the community that has inspired me.

I find constant inspiration that gives me hope, love, and confirmation that I am doing what I'm supposed to be doing. Even my family is starting to come around bit by bit. My mom recently said to me, "Go do all the things. Go learn all the things." This is her way of saying she supports me. Although it's not easy working in this industry, I know that the number of roles I book does not define if I am an artist or not. A painter is not vindicated by the number of paintings sold. It's not about saying yes to everything that comes our way, either. Along with many fellow actors I know, I have turned down roles that were offered to me. At times we say no to the smaller roles because we know we are worthy of the bigger ones.

Recent studies have shown how casting more minorities can bring in higher gross income at global box offices, higher return on investments, and higher ratings in TV. UCLA did a study of the top theatrical films from 2011 to 2016. It showed films that had casts of 21 to 40 percent minorities brought in the highest earnings, at times tripling the earnings of films that had only 10 percent or fewer minorities.

In 2016, out of the 173 films released in the international market, films that had a 20 percent or less cast of minorities had the lowest global box office earnings. In the 2015-2016 television season, broadcast scripted shows that had 10 percent or fewer minorities had the lowest ratings. Gone are the days when minorities can be ignored.

I'm in awe of the trendsetters, the rule breakers, the ones that continuously show us a different perspective on how things can be done. I applaud those who stand up and speak out. Saying something is not always easy. Actress and comedian Margaret Cho has said, "Racism is one of the biggest taboos in our culture, yet most discrimination against Asian Americans goes largely unnoticed." The more awareness we can create, the more change we can make.

To make Hollywood more diverse, we need more diverse staff, from the producers to directors and writers. We need women in all roles as well. Writing is the foundation of a project. The script determines who is in a story and what they do. A female ethnic character written by a female ethnic writer can create a winning, authentic movie or TV show. A diverse staff enriches the screenplay, primarily if it's targeting certain cultures.

I am grateful for the fantastic representation we have in the industry. To all the Sandra Ohs, Mindy Kalings, Maggie Qs, Jon Chos, Daniel Dae Kims, Aziz Ansaris, Margaret Chos, Dev Patels, Constance Wus, Priyanka Chopras, Jackie Chans, Michelle Yeohs, Ang Lees, John M. Chus, Ali Wongs, Steven Yeuns, Jamie Chungs, Ken Jeongs, Cathy Yans, and--of course--Lucy Lius. To every single Asian who has graced the stage, television, and film. To every single Asian behind the scenes. You have inspired me to be better, to do better, and to keep pushing.

CHAPTER 10

BUSINESS VALUE OF INCLUSION

By **JESSIE WANG**

Introduction

"If you do not intentionally include, you will unintentionally exclude."

I have a confession: I love work. In the chaos and uncertainty of life, I've always found solace in organizational charts, key performance indicators, and actionable items. I love knowing that if I continue to learn and work at something, I will find recognition for the effort that I put into it.

I know that this feeling of receiving due recognition for work completed is not necessarily representative of everyone's reality.

Women still make 82 cents for every dollar a man earns. Hispanic workers are 16.7 percent of the workforce but only hold only 6.8 percent of computer and mathematics jobs. Asians are the largest racial cohort of professionals, yet they are the least likely to make managers or executives across all industries. I will only speak to what I know, merging two of the worlds that I inhabit: being an Asian American and being a minor workaholic.

My Background

I am the child of immigrants and an immigrant myself. When I was 6 years old, my parents moved to America and all of a sudden, my birthday, July 4th, was also America's birthday and I was forever labeled as an Asian American.

Since then, I've gone through phases in understanding what that term could mean and fitting into different cultural contexts. Visiting relatives in China, I was branded American. Spending Sundays at Chinese school, I was branded Chinese American. Eating foods that had no clear Romanized name, I was branded Chinese. Walking around the streets of Hong Kong, I was branded a Chinese Mainlander. Working in China, I was branded an "expat." All of these identities feel true and impossible for me to leave behind even if I wanted to.

Asians in the Workplace

"Asians" is a term that encompasses people from such a wide range of geographies that it is not always clear who should count as Asian. Our experiences cover generations, ranging from the founding of America to new immigrants who arrive every day. Our languages and cultures are incredibly diverse, as dialects founded in neighboring regions are unrecognizable to one another.

Despite the fact that Asians are recognized as people of color and as a minority group in American culture at large, the common perception in the technology industry is that Asians are overrepresented and therefore there is no need for formalized structures that recognize or represent Asians. This type of assumption is pervasive in both Asian and non-Asian communities alike. And even today, there remains a question as to why we need to discuss Asian issues in the first place--if Asian issues exist at all.

Statements such as, "Asians make up most of Silicon Valley!" or "Yahoo is almost 40 percent Asian!" gloss over the fact that formal recognition of Asians in companies has value beyond the realm of broadening the number of "diversity hires." This recognition also influences the development of employees, the community, and the underlying business of a company.

Despite the number of diverse people you hire, diversity doesn't thrive when there is no company culture that allows it to. Companies and employees need to make an active effort to recognize that if Asian employees aren't included in decision-making, a group that has been historically considered a silent minority will continued to be ignored.

In this space, employee resource groups (ERGs) have the opportunity to facilitate many of the benefits that come with recognizing Asian employees. From an employee development standpoint, ERGs support retention. In shared spaces, employees can often find individuals that hold similar beliefs and come from similar backgrounds. Informally, I have seen this happen through language lunches. Having lived abroad for close to three years, opportunities to continue to use a language brings together a surprising amount of people who have at some point been expatriates. Recently, some companies have also hosted screenings of movies such as Crazy Rich Asians. Mixed into the comedy, there is also something vulnerable about sharing a movie about a part of the world that you identify with, with your cultural references portrayed on the big screen. Furthermore, for companies with an international presence, ERGs allow international employees to get plugged in and are an easy way to connect.

Secondly, ERGs benefit the communities that companies inhabit. Companies take up land and resources and often shape the course of the communities they are based in. As a result, ERGs allow for a stronger connection between the community and businesses by creating opportunities for companies to give back. At the start of our program, by bringing in community groups, we were able to offer our space, time, and personnel for community events without developing our own set of events, allowing both parties to do what they do best. We've also been able to strengthen the company brand and increase our exposure to populations that may not have familiarity with our business.

And lastly, this type of inclusion is beneficial for the bottom line of a company. By building leaders who can share insights about their communities and knowledge domains, companies can build products that serve all populations. In product development and user experience design, we should focus on building for edge cases and thinking beyond the obvious consumer. And this process should also include identifying communities that have needs that are poorly served.

Companies can't support every single employee individually, but they can create spaces and groups for employees to be supports for each other. While employee resource groups are mostly run by employees, HR teams and senior leadership also have the prerogative to help build out that mission. Companies can provide support for ERGs through budgets, institutional support systems, and processes.

Concluding Thoughts

I have always lived my life under the pretense that I would have a seat at the table. Even though I grew up in a community of predominantly first-generation immigrants, I was always surrounded by managers, doctors, lawyers, or engineers. And as a second-generation immigrant there was little doubt that the expectations for me were even higher. How could you not excel when you were able to learn English before you were middle aged, when you grew up without seeing a civil war?

In college, I demanded leadership positions, took on internships, met regularly with campus administration. I faced few impediments. So as I transitioned into the workplace it never occurred to me that things would be any different. But now, looking back, I am much more aware that many of the same people that I watched build their careers within some of the biggest companies in America ended up leaving those same companies for lack of opportunity to excel and grow, choosing instead to form their own companies where they would control their own destinies.

My workplace is a place that I am proud to tell people about. In an era when work dominates a vast amount of our time, our workplace is often where we learn about the world and interact with new people. It is critical that we set the right standards for diversity and build in messages around inclusion. For Asian Americans, these are opportunities for us to push for greater support systems and for recognition within our workplaces. I want to be part of creating a workspace that recognizes me for who I am and for the work that I bring to the table.

CHAPTER 11

EMPOWERMENT THROUGH ENTERTAINMENT

By MINJI CHANG

There is a beautiful and simple honesty in a child's love for play and make-believe. It baffles me how a unique soul can be revealed at such a young age. I look back on my own childhood and laugh at how obvious it was that I was a pop culture fiend, movie critic, thespian, and business woman by the age of 5.

From as early as 3 years old, I remember singing along to Debbie Gibson, Boyz II Men, Paula Abdul, and MC Hammer. I watched E.T., Top Gun, and every Disney movie under the sun. I teared up when I was moved, screamed when frightened, and provided endless unsolicited commentary on why certain characters, stories, and themes were better than others. I was masterful at playing "house"--I delegated parts, managed props, set agendas for that particular session, and of course, performed my part of mommy (or daddy, sister, dog) with earnest commitment.

I began performing in plays and musicals when I was 5 years old at the Baptist church my family attended. I played the villainous Shirley in "Little Christmas Lamb" and I got my first lead as Candy in the titular "Pop Candy" musical. I coached my older brother on his lines, and although I was an exceptionally shy child in most public settings, I performed my solos with unabashed gusto in front of more than 100 people in the congregation. I moved on to community theater and proceeded to grow in my love and appreciation for the Korean language by being a part of the ensemble cast for Korean Cinderella, which took me up and down California and even to Seoul, Korea. My burgeoning career as a performing artist was rounded out by my love for drawing, coloring, crafts, and writing. And K-Pop. Lots and lots of 90s K-Pop.

Despite all this indulgence in abstract worlds of emotions and make believe, I was quite a good student. I found that I had no need for the stereotypes of tiger parents, as my own standards were grounded in a firm "4.0 or bust." I grew up in the San Francisco bay area and attended public schools in Cupertino, a sleepy part of Silicon Valley blessed with technology much earlier on than the rest of the world was (thanks, Steve Jobs). I was happily schooled at an accelerated rate and played among friends who looked like me and also with many who didn't. I was constantly surrounded by Asian, Latino, African, and Caucasian American peers in a very progressive and diverse part of the world. Gradually my Asian identity was an increasing point of celebration and self-exclusion as I grew older.

My adolescence aligned with the post-1992 Rodney King riots that shook the United States, when racial tensions ran high with resounding ripple effects across generations and ethnicities. Later I'd learn how the conversation centered around the black versus white dynamic in Los Angeles and didn't include Asians ,even though the destruction was centered in Koreatown with Koreans and other Asian business owners. Though I didn't learn about the riots until much later in my life, the "Azn Pride" era of the late 90s and early 2000s ended up being incredibly influential in my pride, confusion, anger, and honoring of my Asian identity.

When you're a teenager trying to figure out who are and how you fit in the grand scheme of things, you cling to any part of your identity that you can take pride in to reconcile that uncomfortable "otherness" feeling. I did so by becoming extra proud of my Asian identity. Azn Pride was a signifier for me to put on a pedestal, a framework for any and all third parties to understand me by. In a world where I was most influenced by what I saw in music, movies, magazines, and TV, this helped me feel like I had some sense of self. Especially, as I came to learn, because I didn't see myself anywhere in my American world.

I recall graduating from Warner Bros. and Disney cartoons to live-action TV, film, and MTV. From "Animaniacs," I moved on to "Saved By The Bell" and "Fresh Prince of Bel Air." In my ongoing love for pop culture, I was as enamored by Zach Morris as I was by Will Smith and all the dreamy boy bands on TRL. I learned about love from "She's All That" and then "Dawson's Creek." I learned about family from "Mrs. Doubtfire" and "Full House" and "Family Matters." I crooned along to Mariah Carey and Whitney Houston, and I grooved to Dru Hill, Blackstreet, Tupac, and Britney Spears. In all these beloved depictions of friendship, love, family, and rebellious coming of age, I didn't see myself at all. The saddest part was, I didn't realize it.

Fast forward to my life in college at UC Berkeley. I was fresh out of a difficult relationship with an older guy. I was already four years into pursuing a career in medicine (helped by a high school health and bioscience career pathway created by my favorite teacher, Mrs. Emerson). But I was facing the challenge of my life, with the goal of majoring in molecular cell biology with a bunch of overachieving STEM geniuses. What was I thinking? My college counselor introduced me to this miraculous new major that fit me like a glove: public health. It was medicine on a grander scale, merging hard science with social science, and applying sociological and psychological analysis to the masses to understand why humans behave the way they do and how this results in health outcomes.

In this transformative and challenging time of my life, degree close to completion, I discovered Kollaboration. This grassroots movement began in 2000 in the heart of Los Angeles by Paul PK Kim, a standup comedian and a corporate lemming turned community rebel who was sick of stereotypical and limited representation of Asians in media. In almost Zuckerberg style, PK put a massive theater rental on his credit card, rallied 13 of his talented Korean American friends--singers, dancers, bboy, and DJs--and put on the very first Kollaboration showcase.

After that inaugural show, the talent showcases expanded to four major cities in North America, growing steadily in reach and influential talent. In 2007, PK and Kollaboration came into my life through a short three-minute video clip that took roughly 24 hours to download on my university DSL connection. In it, PK sang a spoof cover of Boyz II Men's "A Song for Mama" aptly named "A Song for Uhmma (Mom)." You know how sometimes you don't know what you're missing until you come face to face with it? I'd gotten a funny, touching glimpse of my identity. I found Kollaboration's website, and my life was changed.

Today, I have spent about a decade of my life committed to building, sharing, managing, and growing the Kollaboration movement across North America. Since the day I established Kollaboration SF while working full-time in an Oakland public health NPO, I discovered an arena in which all my aptitudes and passions converged. I discovered a purpose plus a means to utilize my analytical, managerial, performing, and creative skillsets. In my tenure at Kollaboration SF and then as global executive director, I was thrown into situations and conversations about race, culture, and self that I couldn't have anticipated, but was always ready to face. As I followed my passion for the arts, my tendency to critically analyze and my need to understand my identity, I found myself. And I found profound value playing a role in a larger movement for authentic and purposeful representation in Hollywood.

Representation is an issue because of the constant attention it requires to include marginalized voices. When powers at be are left to their own devices (and when the powers that be themselves lack diversity), things naturally fall by the wayside. In complacency, oppression can be left to thrive. It's a natural flow of power. If we've learned anything from the lessons provided by books, painting, plays, poems, films, photos and music (you know, art), it's that the status quo must always be challenged. Multiple perspectives are an asset only if we allow them to be so, instead of a hindrance. Through great art we can explore other worlds, fantasy or real, and develop ideas, solutions, and innovations that would otherwise be impossible. And when we make space for others to be represented, to welcome them to the table, to allow them to be heard and be seen, we create that which is sought at the root of all art and humanity--connection.

Kollaboration changed my life by showing me how much representation matters not just in fulfilling quotas and making certain audiences happy, but in the honesty it creates. A few years into my stint as Kollaboration SF director, I revived my longing to pursue acting. Being around all these artists year after year, supporting their work and promoting their creative works to invigorate the community--it was now my turn. Would I walk my own talk, would I take the leap, would I have the hard and disappointing conversations with my parents, would I endure the rejection, would I find a way to raise my voice for myself and for stories that didn't seem to matter at that point? The answer was a giant hell yes. To be fair, that first hell yes was more of a fiery whisper in my heart rather than a Tarzan yell from a rooftop. But that's all it took. Kollaboration was birthed from one tiny show for a handful of friends at a university theater: sometimes all you need is a small declaration to start shaking off invisible shackles and commit to becoming the best version of yourself.

I credit all the amazing independent artists, YouTube creators, and Asian celebrities who came into my life during Kollaboration shows for stoking my fire and allowing me to dare to dream. I credit my big brother who had the shrewd and loving perception to ask me if medicine was really my biggest dream or if there was something more out there for me. Until I was in my 20s, I had a hard time naming a single Asian American actress or superstar. What PK had pointed out in Kollaboration was true: that not seeing something being done made it feel impossible or simply absent from any of our realities. Hollywood was fixed in my mind as some foreign planet that I was not welcome on, a place I did not have the means to reach. I've learned time and time again the importance of role models and mentors to help grow and expand opportunities.

Hollywood is an incredibly important nut to crack in terms of diversity, and it will be my life's work to crack that nut, whether it's in front of a camera or in an office. Why? I Think about how much I still remember the gentle comedy of Steve Urkel and the transformation of Cher from Clueless. The images we see, the stories that are told, the hashtags that go viral, and the heroes that we treasure will continue to play some of the most sacred and influential roles in our lives. Arts and media are incredibly powerful tools for setting our sights higher, being more empathetic individuals, becoming more in touch with our humanity, and transforming into better citizens of the world. If we can do it more consciously, I'm on board.

I believe diversity in arts and media can best be supported by the organizational policies of different social movements like #TimesUp and #RepresentationMatters. Although it might feel fluffy (yet another hashtag), it can actually result in structural strategy and hiring processes that create authentic diversity and inclusion. It's ambitious to think it can be nailed on the first try, so I think a major lesson of mine in the last decade has been to plan with patience and persistence. There must be room for iterations and constructive feedback so we can continuously grow and improve.

I've witnessed the proliferation of diversity programs from every major studio who are seeking diverse voices in the writer's rooms, acting roles, and directorial positions. These are all phenomenal starts, and I believe it must expand from there. We cannot discount the importance of inclusion at all levels of production and professional capacities, including casting, cinematography, makeup, finance, production, and more. The creative genius made from a unique eye is more valuable that any quota could define. This is why my pursuit of an acting career has led me down the road of writing, because I understand that the true voice from my many backgrounds (Korean American, female, millennial, Californian, geeky artist) is best when spoken from the source.

The future of diversity and inclusion is a mix of creating space and opportunities and being willing to risk embarrassment and failure by putting our authentic voices out there to be heard and for our true selves to be seen. I applaud any and every person who takes on this important and worthy goal. I look forward to working with you.

CHAPTER 12

THE STORY OF AN AUSTRALIAN ASIAN

By **NEIL YEOH**

I was 5 years old when I realized I was different from other kids. My mom was picking me up from school one evening when she called me to come over. I was with my two friends and they gave me the most confusing stare. I wanted my friends to meet my mom, but they didn't move. Did they not hear her?

I didn't realize it at the time, but my mom changed between speaking Cantonese and English so frequently in my childhood that sometimes I couldn't tell the difference. That's the reason my white friends couldn't understand when she spoke Cantonese. I thought they were acting up, but really it was because of my cultural difference.

My parents were first-generation Asian immigrants who moved to Australia during the late 1980s. My mother fled Shanghai when she was a child, becoming a refugee in Hong Kong before the Cultural Revolution, and my father grew up in a second-generation Malaysian Chinese family during the tin mining boom. They were both sent to England to study in their teens, met, and got married after a few years of dating between London and Sunderland. They had my sister and brother in England, but after a few tough years scraping by, they migrated to Australia in search of a better life.

My parents' move to Australia was not easy. My father's job at the local hospital meant my mother had to watch my sister and brother in the nurses' residence where our family initially stayed. Knowing no one in the city, my mother would spend most of her time in isolation with my brother and sister, as my father worked long hours. The one thing that would always make my mother smile were the jacaranda trees that would bloom with beautiful purple flowers during the spring.

However, my parents eventually adapted to their new surroundings. Mom found a local Asian immigrant church for us to attend, building a community of friends around us. Dad eventually earned enough for a down payment on a house behind a winery on the northeast foothills of the city where I would eventually grow up.

I was never part of the plan: my mom calls me a "surprise gift" from God. My early childhood was typical of many western-born Asians. I started classical piano at 8 years old, went to Saturday Chinese class until my early teens, and attended after school math classes for 6 years. Misbehavior was met with a bamboo cane, and academic excellence, obedience, and respect of elders were ingrained into my existence.

When I was growing up, there was little choice but to assimilate into the local culture. Outside the safety net of my family and Asian church community, I was an ethnic minority. At primary school I was one of only a handful of Asians. Assimilation was not something that came easily. By the time we learned about ethnic cultures in school, classmates referred to me as a "chink," with the tune "Ching Chong Chinaman" ringing in the distance, sung by strange kids as I walked to class. But kids are kids, and neither my friends nor I knew the concept of racism at the time.

I had bullies. Our school uniform was maroon, and all kids had to wear hats during recess and lunch. All kids' hats were maroon, but my mom insisted I wear a hand-me-down white wide-brimmed hat from my brother. That hat became a visual target on my head worsened by my ethnicity. It wasn't long until three guys from two years above me began to target me. They would push and shove me to the point where I would dread leaving the classroom.

I don't think I ever told my parents, although I'm not sure why. Perhaps it was because I was afraid of getting in trouble for causing trouble. But my friends stood up for me. I remember one lunchtime when my best friend Caspar led my friends in standing up to the bullies, thus ending their interest in chasing me. It is a vivid image baked into my memory. My white friends standing up against my white bullies showed me that there was nothing wrong with being different, a truth upheld by my friends who saw beneath the surface of my skin to who I was--a friend they cared for beyond my ethnicity.

I carried this image throughout my life, and without realizing it, I became slow to judge people. Growing up with dual cultures meant I could empathize with and relate to many others from different cultures and backgrounds. In my senior year of high school, this quality saw me elected as the first Asian head perfect in the 90-year history of the school. It wasn't because I was any special kind of leader, but I had friends from all walks of life. I didn't let the high school silos of different social groups define who I could or couldn't be friends with. Seeing beyond the surface of someone's skin and ethnic background became the reason why I was elected to represent the collective voice of our school community. Cultural diversity speaks.

As an Asian, I was hardwired to seek approval in everything I did. I would constantly seek approval from my parents, to hear them say, "I am proud of you." Our family never spoke openly about our emotions or feelings, and my parents tried to shelter us from the sacrifices they had to make to provide for us. It was our job as Asian kids to get good grades, get into a good college, graduate with a good degree, and find a good job. For my formative years I followed this convention and graduated with engineering and business degrees before starting work in Perth, Western Australia as a management consultant.

When I started my job, I didn't know how cultural biases and hardwiring would influence me in the workplace. I blindly trusted and respected authority and hierarchy in my early career, listening and doing exactly what I was told. This worked for a while in getting me staffed on projects and building a reputation as a reliable and hardworking team member. However, it wasn't long until I started getting staffed on a series of repetitive and monotonous projects. I spoke up, but the partner and manager strongly advised me to stick with it and wait for a promotion. I stayed on these projects for nine months too long, learning little yet earned revenue for the organization. During our annual review, I got a top performance ranking but was not promoted. I returned to the partner and manager and they told me to stick at the project for longer. Yet after another six months, nothing changed. It was a carrot on a stick held just out of my reach.

At the same time, I had a colleague who went against the advice of the partners and worked his way through the system. Against the wishes of our local partners, he ended up negotiating a transfer to Sydney and later a promotion. Meanwhile, I remained obedient and hardworking in my local roles. I became jaded when I realized that the partners and managers didn't have my best interests in mind. My cultural hardwiring had blinded me from the harsh realities of the corporate world. After two and a half years, I ended up leaving to join a boutique strategy-consulting firm in Sydney.

Our boutique firm was acquired by one of the big four accounting firms after a year and a half of hard work and growth. I remember entering the boardroom with our new managing director, who wanted to address the five of us who would be joining the firm. I was a senior consultant at the time, as was my colleague who sat beside me that day. The managing director gave a typical speech and then turned to us and explained that there were many opportunities at the firm for more senior employees (gesturing at my colleague) and graduates (gesturing at me). It was a completely innocent remark and yet it sticks so clearly in my mind. It was the first time in my life where I felt uncomfortable with someone assuming I was younger and more junior than I actually was. I realized my appearance should not affect my seniority or how others perceive my capabilities. Learning from past experiences, I worked hard to get staffed on interesting projects and spoke up when I needed to-- hoping my efforts would overcome any biases I would face.

When I met with my performance manager and told him my plans of being promoted to manager, he advised me to be patient and wait it out for at least a year and take on more projects. It was already difficult for me to envision myself as a manager, as few managers in the office looked like me. I felt deflated but found the right encouragement and validation from my project manager to not give up. He told me that he already saw me as a capable manager, and that I just had to see it and believe it myself. I realized that if I couldn't see it myself then no one would. After I read our company policy, I learned I could choose my performance manager, so I chose a manager who believed in and supported my aspirations. I met with the partner of my division and asked for an early review for promotion to manager. She agreed, and before I knew it I had received the top ranking at my level and received an off-cycle early promotion to manager. I untied the stick and ate the carrot.

However, my pathway up until this point was relatively conventional. Culturally I was allowed to dream, but only within certain boundaries. I remember when I was a child and my parents asked me who I wanted to be when I grew up. I mentioned that I wanted to be the piano player at the departmental store, sharing endless music to bypassing shoppers. I was told that I could do that perhaps when I retired. I harbor no negativity towards this response as it part of the Asian immigrant story--to want better for the next generation. Ironically, I believe that many Asians harbor great talent and potential that are not realized given cultural pressures to conform to convention and expectations. My life at this point was no different.

The turning point in my career came when I decided to go to graduate school. Despite corporate success I felt unfulfilled, wanting to use my skills and experience in a career with social purpose. I wasn't afraid of change, but I was risk-adverse, a quality baked into my cultural psyche. It was hard to leave my job to pursue my true social passions because it also meant breaking away from the cultural values I learnt. I spent a lot of time in self-reflection focusing on the imprint I wanted to have on this world. It was one of the first times I intentionally questioned my existence beyond what was expected of me. I found comfort and safety in work, but I was drawn to something more.

After searching for an answer, I eventually landed on a phrase that to this day still guides my personal vision: "to see a world where our gifts are used to their fullest potential and for the greatest good." It has become my personal driving force extending beyond my cultural ethnicity or values and speaking to the fundamental truth of who I want to be on this earth.

I came to graduate school at Oxford with a polished demeanor, trained through consulting to speak with intention, concision, and confidence. While overcoming my cultural hardwiring, I had built an impenetrable front-facing persona so that no one could question my capabilities. It was a façade and separated my work from my life. It wasn't until I got to know my classmates from so many different walks of lives, cultures, and countries that things changed. Cultural diversity was more than the isolated experiences I had in Adelaide, Perth, and Sydney. I need not hide my cultural insecurities, as my differences reflect my unique strengths. Cultural diversity--with all its good and bad--is something to be accepted and embraced. In an environment where cultural diversity is valued, I was able to open up and bring my whole self. Before long, the façade I built to compensate for my perceived cultural flaws faded away as I embraced who I am both inside and out.

The energy that I channeled toward maintaining a certain image of worthiness was freed. I was able to confront my insecurities and embrace them. I was able to focus on what realizing my potential and my social purpose really meant. I was able to work on eliminating my doubts and fears, like caring about what others may think. I channeled my energy into exploring two career pathways to a career of social purpose: consulting in international development and working to tackle climate change. The first took me to Nairobi, Kenya, where I worked with Dalberg for an agricultural technology startup helping smallholder farmers. The second took me to New York, which is where I now work in 2018 with Echoing Green as the deputy director of individual fellow support and climate portfolio.

I can share my story today with authenticity and conviction because I accept both my cultural upbringing and myself completely, finding belongingness in this world of diverse individuals. I know that I am not alone, that my experience resonates with many people from different upbringings, cultures, and countries. Today,

I wake up every day excited and driven to do the work that I do--tackling climate change through investing in and incubating climate solutions and supporting social entrepreneurs. I found a workplace that puts diversity, equity, and inclusion at the heart of the organization, a place where I can bring my full self. I live in a city where differences are celebrated, where pursuing a cause bigger than myself is welcomed.

As I reflect back on my conservative upbringing to who I am today, I cannot help but feel gratitude about being an Australian Asian. It has given me the cultural awareness to relate to so many people, the resilience to adapt to and perform in the workplace, and the courage to break away from risk adversity and bring my full self to everything that I do, including my social purpose today.

CHAPTER 13

THE DHANDHO PHILOSOPHY

By SHAAN PATEL

I grew up in a cramped two-bed, one-bathroom living space in my parents' rundown Las Vegas motel that was frequented by drug addicts, prostitutes, and police. I remember when I was 6 years old walking in flip-flops along my cracked "neighborhood" sidewalk trying to avoid shattered glass from broken beer bottles. Although I was too embarrassed to invite friends over, I was lucky enough to have loving parents who adhered to Indian cultural values of tolerance, hard work, and most importantly, education. My mom always said that they would spend money on "two things--school and food."

After volunteering at a local emergency department when I was in high school, I was inspired to become a physician. When

I learned about combined baccalaureate/M.D. programs that offered high school students a guaranteed spot in medical school, I decided that's what I wanted. However, these programs had an average acceptance rate of 5 percent and SAT score of 2250. After receiving a 1760 on my first practice SAT, I spent countless hours studying at the library to raise my score to a perfect 2400. But my reluctance to share the upbringing I had been ashamed of as a child led to sub-par applications that didn't convey my authentic story. I was rejected multiple times before I was finally accepted into the University of Southern California's combined BS/MD program on a full scholarship.

Because students in BS/MD programs are encouraged to explore interests outside of medicine, I pursued writing an SAT prep book to help other students prepare for the SAT the way that I did in high school. Unfortunately, most literary agents and publishers dismissed my book proposal. (One wrote, "I didn't find Shaan's writing or persona particularly engaging--he's not a great writer, no matter what his score is.") After writing hundreds of pages, I had two options: continue to hope for a book deal or give up. But when you don't like Plan A or Plan B ... make Plan C. I used extra scholarship money I had saved as initial capital to launch Prep Expert SAT Prep. The 376-point average score improvement (equivalent to taking a student's score from the 50th to the 90th percentile) in the pilot SAT class I taught confirmed that my "easy-to-read" text actually resonated quite well with high school students.

When McGraw-Hill, the world's largest educational publisher, saw what I was building, the acquisitions editor offered me a book deal. Proving my expertise paid off. I spent just as many hours in the same library during the summer of 2011 writing my SAT prep book as I did during the summer of 2006 studying for the SAT. The only difference was that in 2006 I was solely concerned about my own future, whereas in 2011 I was concerned about the future of thousands of students.

When I was in medical school at USC, I wanted to develop an online SAT course. But there was one problem: McGraw-Hill now owned the copyright to my material. When I began contacting online test prep providers, one potential partner said, "It won't be possible to use that material in online SAT prep ... you've backed yourself into a corner." But I didn't let this rejection stop me from finding an escape out of that corner. After meeting the founders of Veritas Prep, we pursued literary licensing until negotiations became stagnant. I then reached out to McGraw-Hill's VP of Global Sales directly and outlined how packaging every online course with a copy of my book, SAT 2400 in Just 7 Steps, would help sell thousands of more books than we had originally projected--and he approved the deal. The book ended up hitting number one on Amazon for SAT Prep and sold more than 50,000 copies!

I continued to challenge defined limits by taking a leave of absence from medical school at USC to attend business school at Yale for a dual purpose: to learn more about healthcare management and to scale my company from a small business in Las Vegas to a national test-prep brand. That leap helped me achieve both goals, and in January of 2016, I appeared on ABC's "Shark Tank."

"I See A Young Tony Robbins."

Billionaire Mark Cuban said this to me during my pitch on "Shark Tank," a television show in which hopeful entrepreneurs pitch their companies to a multibillionaire panel of business magnates for an investment. I went on the show to pitch my test-prep company Prep Expert that offers six-week SAT and ACT prep classes in 20 cities and online. I ended up securing a deal with Mark Cuban for $250,000 in exchange for 20 percent equity in my company.

But the ultimate compliment was not Mark Cuban's investment, but what he said about me. He waited until all four of the other Sharks rejected my proposal for an investment to speak about what he envisioned for me. He thought that I had a bigger vision than test-prep, that I would start multiple companies in the future. He said he would like to do an "acqui-hire"--investing in a company to recruit its employees (in this case, me). When I said Prep Expert was my "baby," Mark Cuban said he would like to be the "Godfather to my future children."

Mark Cuban gave me the ultimate endorsement. He wanted to invest in me, not just my company. There's no clause in my contract that states I must give Mark Cuban 20 percent of my future ventures. Instead, we have a handshake deal that says I will give Mark Cuban an option to invest in any other company I launch. And why wouldn't I want that option? I believe 80 percent of any company in partnership with Mark Cuban is more valuable than 100 percent of a company by myself.

I think Cuban saw a little bit of himself in me. He sold his first company, Microsolutions, for $6 million in 20TK. After taking some time to travel the world, he then started Broadcast.com (formerly

Audionet) and sold it for $6 billion to Yahoo! You've got to hit a single before you can hit a homerun. Perhaps Cuban thinks that Prep Expert is my single, and he's just waiting to be a part of my homerun.

Mark Cuban also said that he thought I was a "young Tony Robbins." This comment served as the inspiration for my contribution to this book. Tony Robbins is the most successful self-help guru in history. His work is inspiring, passionate, and downright life-changing. For Mark Cuban to put me in the same bracket as Tony Robbins is immensely flattering. If my story here can be half as inspiring as those in Robbins' books, I'd be elated.

Some people succeed financially. Others succeed academically. Still others succeed spiritually, mentally, and emotionally. But there are a select few who succeed across all fields--the self-made successes.

By the age of 25, I had accomplished a lot: I'd achieved a perfect SAT score, was valedictorian and homecoming king, received a quarter-million dollars in college scholarships, grew a business from nothing to a seven figure-valuation from my dorm room, had a multimillionaire Lamborghini-driving business partner and a multibillionaire NBA-team owning business partner, wrote seven bestselling books, was the youngest recipient of Las Vegas' 40 Under 40 Awards, and had been featured on more than 100 media and television channels, including Forbes, USA Today, and The New York Times. I did this all while dissecting cadavers at a top-tier medical school in California and attending an Ivy League graduate business school in Connecticut.

I have worked for everything I have achieved. Personally, I hate taking handouts. I grew up in my parents' urban motel in Las Vegas and attended inner-city public schools in the worst school district in the nation with a 40 percent dropout rate. I believe that the circumstances surrounding your upbringing should not limit you.

So can you really have it all at a young age? Yes. Throw out the conventional wisdom that says you have to pay your dues or climb the corporate ladder. You can have it all and you can have it now.

I certainly could've taken the road well-travelled and sat on my perfect SAT score. But I found an empty market niche and leveraged my assets to develop an effective curriculum that helped students improve their academic futures.

Much of my success is due to my Asian-American background-- specifically Indian, or Gujarati. The principles I learned growing up in a Gujarati household were crucial to the successes I have described above. One such is the principle of "Dhandho."

"Dhandho" is a Gujarati word that means "endeavors that create wealth." To practice Dhandho philosophy means taking a low-risk, high-reward approach to business, investment, saving, and spending.

I first learned about Dhandho philosophy when a friend told me that I should read Mohnish Pabrai's The Dhandho Investor. While the book is primarily about value investing, Pabrai also describes a group of people that have used the Dhandho philosophy most effectively: Patel motel-owners. With little education or capital,

Patels immigrated to the United States in the late twentieth century and began applying the Dhandho philosophy to their businesses. They now own more than $40 billion in hospitality-associated assets in the USA and employ over a million people.

Although I have been immersed in Dhandho philosophy my entire life, I never knew what it was called. It has been deeply ingrained in the culture of Gujaratis. As a child, I used to think my parents were just being "cheap." For example, my mom would never allow me to get a soda from Taco Bell because we had soda at home. Although taking frugality to this level might sound ridiculous, this practice of saving is part of larger Dhandho philosophy that has led to massive wealth for many Indian Americans. According to the U.S. Census Bureau, Indian Americans are the wealthiest ethnic group in America.

The power of Dhandho philosophy increases exponentially when it is applied to business. Mark Cuban definitely practices Dhandho philosophy. Cuban is famous for saying, "Only morons start a business on a loan." What he is saying is do not start something as high-risk as a new business with something as high-risk as a loan, a perfect example of Dhandho philosophy in practice.

Cuban chose to go to Indiana University because it had the least expensive tuition. Similarly, I chose to go to USC because they gave me a full-tuition scholarship. Mark used to sleep on the floor in college, with a closet as his room. I chose to take the smallest room in our three-bedroom apartment at Yale so that I would only have to spend $500/month on rent--just $6,000 a year for housing! Of course, you need to balance frugality with enjoying life. But most people do way too much of the latter and not enough of the former.

There are only two ways to become wealthy: Make more money or spend less money. Doing both of these together can have powerful effects. To make more money, build value to create passive income streams. To spend less money, practice Dhandho philosophy in all aspects of your life.

For example, when I wanted to start Prep Expert in college, I ran into a chicken-and-egg problem. I needed to have a location to run classes to advertise on the website, but I didn't want to lease a location until I had a few student enrollments to cover my costs of leasing a location.

What do you think most people would have done in my situation? They might take out a business loan to secure a short-term lease on a retail location, rent temporary furniture like classroom desks, and hire a receptionist to staff the location in case parents wanted to drop in.

But I was a college student who had $900 left over from my scholarships to start this business. I'd never taken a loan in my life and I wasn't about to take one to start my business. So I channeled my Indian immigrant heritage's Dhandho philosophy and found another way.

I came across executive office co-working spaces. These locations typically have conference rooms that seat 10 to 15 people, which are equipped with whiteboards and large LCD TVs.

In addition, they have receptionists staffed at the location during business hours to help any parents that may drop in to look at the location.

The best part was that I could rent the conference room only for the hours that I needed it. This meant that I would not have the overhead costs of leasing, furnishing, and staffing my own location. Applying Dhandho philosophy allowed me to save thousands of dollars that other test prep companies waste.

In business, practice Dhandho philosophy by finding alternatives to loans to fund your idea. Most Internet businesses can be started for little to no capital because of the plethora of free and cheap web tools available. If your business does require a significant amount of capital to start it, try to save enough money from your current job, find a new job to generate income to fund your idea, start a crowd-funding campaign, or consider a less capital-intensive business altogether.

So what does diversity and inclusion mean to me? In business, I believe more Asian-Americans should hold management positions at Fortune 500 Companies. By applying cultural principles, such as Dhandho philosophy, I believe American businesses will benefit from higher revenue, lower costs, and ultimately greater profits.

CHAPTER 14

A KOREAN AMERICAN ENTREPRENEUR'S STORY

By STELLA SONG

Train cars rushed past as I sat in the metro station waiting for my train to arrive. As I watched the trains go by, I sat up straighter. There was an advertisement on the side of each train car, and together, they formed a flipbook-style story of the product. I was brought back to my preschool years when sitting in the laundromat, I had formulated a similar idea to be used during the revolutions of washing machines and dryers. Now, two decades later, here was my first business idea come to reality. My preschool mind had seen a possibility that is now commonplace—use technology to engage people during a dull situation.

Many people talk about passion, but that's never been my motivator. Even as a child, I was obsessed with the idea of reaching my fullest potential and knowing my truest capabilities. My parents are Korean immigrants, which meant I grew up between two cultures and between two generations. Korea struggled economically in the early eighties, which led my parents to immigrate to the United States, along with many other Koreans. Working with my dad's family in Los Angeles, my mother was marginalized and often shunted aside. Instead of accepting this, she founded her own store in the fashion industry with my father's support. For two people who didn't speak English and had no concept of marketing, their success story is the embodiment of the American Dream. I had a front-row seat to their struggle and success.

Growing Up Korean and American

I was raised in traditional Korean culture, brought up with the understanding that I was supposed to take care of others above myself. Throughout my childhood and teenage years, I often thought that my parents' conservative way of parenting would scar me emotionally. As a bicultural child, I felt stifled by them. Korean culture has a history of valuing boys more than girls, although I didn't recognize this until later on in life. Looking back, I realize that my little brother was favored. But even with my family's clear preference toward my brother, I never internalized this dynamic. Instead, I relied on my ideas and resources to pave my path and parent myself. I extricated myself from my family dynamic and moved to Paris for college, where I was able to create my own rules and begin with a blank slate, not being bound by cultural norms.

The hardship of my parents' life in the U.S. has always been clear to me. They worked in a very competitive and homogenous industry. Everyone I knew working in fashion manufacturing was

Korean, and the pressures of competing against the same people who should be supporting each other through the struggle of immigration and scarcity impacted me profoundly. I feel a great deal of compassion for my parents and the people they are today. It must have been terrifying for them to come to a country where they didn't speak the language and have to learn how to operate in a new society. Their success in the fashion industry and the fact that they were able to enroll me at an expensive private school speaks to the grit and determination of their generation. I can't recall them ever complaining, only consistently working and doing their best for the family.

Growing up Korean meant confronting not just cultural challenges, but also racism. I realize now how naïve I was about the racism my family faced. Once on a family vacation when we were kids, my brother, family friends, and I were at the pool when a group of kids came up to us. They pulled the skin next to their eyes back and stuck their tongues out. We didn't know what was happening, so we made the same face back. Later, we did it in front of our parents. Instead of explaining the gesture, they told us to put our hands over our noses to make a big nose. We were confused but played along. Later, I realized that we were both making racist faces.

Another time, I was helping my mom at her store, and a woman came up to me and called me a moon face. I thought it was a compliment because the moon is beautiful. However, when I told my teacher about it at school, she reprimanded me for repeating it. It took me years to understand it. Then, as now, it didn't make any sense to me that people would attack somebody for their appearance.

Once I entered high school, everyone seemed to gravitate toward their own ethnic groups. If I tried to befriend a Hispanic girl, they would ask, "What are you doing? You belong in the Asian group, in the Korean group." Even within the Korean group, I had to choose between the "FOBs" (Fresh Off The Boat), who were born and raised in Korea and then moved to the U.S., or the "Itaewaons," who were American-born. How was I supposed to choose? Culturally, I related to both the FOBs and the Itaewaons, thanks to my upbringing in a strict Korean household and my exposure to American culture through television and school.

After high school, I moved to Paris to study at the American University of Paris. It was my first time living and traveling abroad. Growing up in what felt like a forced racially segregated friend group reinforced my desire to be a global citizen. Upon finishing college, I moved to New York and then returned to Paris, where I was able to build my life without the expectation that I would only socialize with people who looked like me. I learned just how similar people are across seemingly significant divides.

Founding Stories

I was always entrepreneurial. My first business idea, which integrated a waiting experience with technology, came to me as a preschooler and I continued to develop ideas throughout my childhood. The first time I made money was in kindergarten. A friend admired the watch I was wearing and asked if he could have it. My first instinct was to give it to him. But then I remembered how hard it was for me to get the watch. My parents had a store on Santee Alley, the wholesale district in Los Angeles, and I would often go with them. I fell in love with this watch, but it was $5, which I did not have. Eventually, I convinced the man selling me the watch to give it to me for a quarter. Back on the playground, as I was about to give my friend the watch, I remembered how hard it was for me to get the watch in the first place. I thought I'd ask for a quarter." But then I had the idea to ask for two quarters so that I could get more watches and then sell those. I went back, got more, and began selling watches during lunch to the other kids. I consider that moment my business epiphany. I remember the feeling of brightness and accomplishment. I was hooked on the idea of building value out of something small or even from a simple concept.

The first company I founded was a clothing manufacturing company in China. I moved to China and worked for free for quite some time while brokering some deals. Eventually, I was able to save up, find a client in the United States, and begin to build my business. Manufacturing is a tough business, even risky. An order comes in, and the firm must produce the item according to its exact specifications. These specifications are why quality control is so vital to the life and success of a manufacturing company. There is an immense pressure to make each item perfect, knowing that failure to have good quality control is the reason so many manufacturing companies fail.

In most cases, I was dealing with Caucasians, who were either buyers or owners of stores. I learned from a white friend who worked in a department store that there was a significant amount of institutionalized racism and stereotyping through association. American department stores that buy from Asia generally operate under the assumption that Asians are untrustworthy, that they might do something devious or shady. I realize now how much more challenging it would have been to begin a company in the U.S. Although it's always distressing to hear about racism, I was grateful to have this knowledge. It made me careful and aware and gave me an advantage as I approached new buyers. It was better to know and determine how to move forward than to run blindly into barriers that are unseen or unknown.

When I started my company, I had no financial support, but what hurt the most was not having emotional support, particularly from my family. In our traditional Korean home, my family raised me with the intention that I would not have to work in my adult life, that I could merely marry and have a family. My mom worked incredibly hard and didn't want me to encounter a similar experience as her. To enter adulthood and reject that life, instead of becoming an entrepreneur and founder, was a refusal of Korean culture and my parents' values.

During the early days of my manufacturing company, my life had many parallels with my parents' story. I was alone, scared, in a new country, and I had my parents' voices continually reinforcing the idea that I was never going to amount to anything, telling me, "You don't know what you're doing. You are worthless." As I began to internalize this narrative, the same spirit that led me to build my world as a child rose up and fought back. I began to think, "If I'm already at rock bottom, the only way to go is up." I began to ask, "What if things were okay?" I came to realize that there would be a day when I have the chance to get out of the situation. When that opportunity presents itself, I want to be ready to enjoy it.

As my entrepreneurial journey continued, a friend approached me to become a business partner in his luxury media company.

With my international presence and ability to run a tight-ship from my experience in manufacturing, he needed someone who could expand the company's presence and take it to the next level. I accepted his offer and entered the luxury and technology sector. In retrospect, I realize how reflecting can inform areas of growth and change. The work was a dramatic switch from the work I had been doing in China. Coming in, I believed that the only thing that mattered was hard work. Working in the field of catering to individuals looking to enjoy a luxurious lifestyle, my negative preconceptions about that lifestyle were altered, and I learned that luxury means different things to each of us.

That experience helped me define my business ethos of authenticity and luxury. For me, authenticity and luxury are not related to money. Your definition of happiness is where your heart, mind, or soul takes you. Being surrounded by good friends, eating simple food, and having great conversations with friends is luxury to me.

Allowing the past to inform my future, even the painful parts, has been one of my biggest life lessons. One of the benefits of remembering the situations from your past is having the hindsight that brings clarity toward what you want for yourself or your business in the present. This clarity can take the form of an idea you have now that you want to add to your business, adding components to a relationship, or recognizing what you don't want to happen again. Although it can be hard to look back on these situations, it always brings me clarity.

Looking Forward

As I have become more involved in other companies, sitting on boards or joining as a partner, I've felt the difficulty of being an Asian-American woman increase. It was easier when I was doing everything myself. I went through a period of personal and spiritual development, which led to working more with other people. While this has included excellent working relationships, when a man is uncomfortable working with women, barriers begin to come up. I work with many alpha-males, and as I seek to accomplish things within partnerships or teams, many men chafe at hearing directions or critique from me. I have dealt with this across cultures, which has led me to develop a theory that when men hear a woman speaking in a critical or even matter-of-fact voice, it brings up memories of being scolded by their mother, leading to a negative reaction.

No matter what industry I'm working in, I hear on a daily basis what others think I should be like, as a woman or boss or daughter or future wife. What often surprises people is that I do what I like and follow what I'm interested in, rather than conforming to another person's ideas. If there's anything I learned growing up Asian American, it's the importance of calling out this mistreatment. I approach these business situations in the same way I approached racism growing up. I call them out. Often, men will try to make you feel awkward or strange that you're behaving a certain way, but it's important to take that pseudo-power away from them, by calling them out on their biases. It's not easy. I can't say any of the things I've done have been easy. Being able to live life on my own terms is what makes it worthwhile for me.

The best advice I can offer you is to spend time outside of your culture. Travel, try different foods, and meet new people, and you will find more similarities than you ever imagined. Growing up in both Korean and American culture, and later living in Paris and China, I've been struck by how similar we all are. No matter where you are or where you come from, we are all looking to be seen, connect, and be in a relationship with one another. Invite your neighbors into your home and spend time with one another. Once you start doing this, it's so much harder to be judgmental or racist.

The second piece of advice I can give is to trust yourself. You are the only one that really can know and make the best decisions for yourself in your own life. If I had followed the path laid out for me by my parents, I would be a wife and a mother who had not worked a day in her life. That was not the path for me. Business thrills me, and it always has--I listened to that thrill from early on in my life. Nothing is better than the advice you can give yourself. I accomplish this by connecting to my internal dialogue and desires through meditation and intentional self-evaluation.

The journey I've taken from a confused kid raised in competing cultures to an entrepreneurial, global businesswoman has not been straightforward. But that's the joy and power of my story. I want to never be complacent, so I'm always looking toward the future, asking how I can challenge myself next. I'm intrigued by the latest advancements in technology and will continue to be on the front lines of integrating these ideas into improving companies. I'll continue to fight for respect and project the strength that only I can bring along the way. I hope that my story inspires another minority woman to trust in herself and give it her all.

CONCLUSION

Diversity and inclusion are not a passing fad. These are important issues that shouldn't have to "go viral" to get your attention because some event or piece of entertainment makes the news or is trending on Twitter. I am grateful for these stories that remind us to be thoughtful and approach life with a new level of understanding for our fellow human beings. These stories are the result of a small group of people coming together to provoke change. This is just one small step.

To make bigger strides, more people need to become aware about issues of diversity and participate in the conversation. I encourage you to keep talking about these issues. Don't just put this book down and go about your normal life. If you are inspired, hold on to that feeling and do something about it. While grand gestures are nice, small ones add up, too. Maybe start by engaging in a conversation with a friend about this book you just read? Share your ideas. An idea without action is just a dream. Make your dream a reality by adding a little action.

To share your stories on business and diversity, connect with me on Instagram @AskAdamTorres

To your success,

Adam Torres

APPENDIX

Adam Torres | Foreword | Page iii
Co-Founder Money Matters Top Tips
Instagram: @AskAdamTorres

Alexander Eng | Chapter 1 | Page 1
Senior Vice President, Market Executive, Commercial Banking,
Bank of America Merrill Lynch
LinkedIn: Alexander Eng

Alice Yi | Chapter 2 | Page 9
Co-Founder
Digital Luxury Agency
alice@digitalluxuryagency.com

Ban Tran | Chapter 3 | Page 19
CEO, Trans International Group
transinternationalgroup.com

Chirag Sagar | Introduction, Chapter 4 | Page v, 29
Co-Founder and COO, Money Matters Top Tips
chirag@MoneyMattersTopTips.com
Instagram: @chiragdsagar
Twitter: @chiragdsagar
LinkedIn: Chiragsagar

Christine Drinan | Chapter 5 | Page 41
Founder and CEO, Galavante
Instagram: @galavantingchristine @galavante
galavante.com

Eva lino | Chapter 6 | Page 49
LinkedIn: Eva lino
Instagram: @eva_x2

Hanna Li | Chapter 7 | Page 59
Founder and Creative Director of Zehana Interiors
Instagram:@ZehanaInteriors
zehana.com
hello@zehana.com

Japman Bajaj | Chapter 8 | Page 67
Twitter: @japman_bajaj
LinkedIn: Japmanbajaj
jb@1469solutions.com

Jeneviere Kim | Chapter 9 | Page 79
Instagram: @jenevierekim

Jessie Wang | Chapter 10 | Page 87
Founder Beijing Women's Network, Global Shaper
LinkedIn: Jessiexwang

Minji Chang| Chapter 11 | Page 93
Actor, Writer, Producer
Instagram: @minjeezy

Neil Yeoh | Chapter 12 | Page 101
Climate Investor, Advocate, Startup Advisor
Instagram: neilyeoh
LinkedIn: www.linkedin.com/in/neilyeoh

Shaan Patel, M.D., M.B.A | Chapter 13 | Page 111
Founder, Prep Expert Test Preparation, author of *Self-Made Success*
selfmadesuccessbook.com

Stella Song | Chapter 14 | Page 121
Co-Founder and CEO, Well Made Collaborations, Inc., Titan Connect
stella@stellasong.com
Instagram: @loveandluxuria

Listen to the
MONEY MATTERS
TOP TIPS PODCAST
where Business Owners, Entrepreneurs and Executives
share their top tips for success!

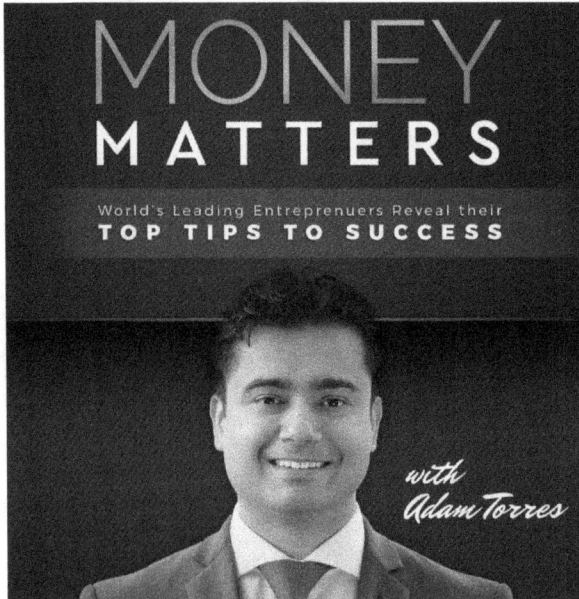

MoneyMattersTopTips.com/podcast

OTHER AVAILABLE TITLES

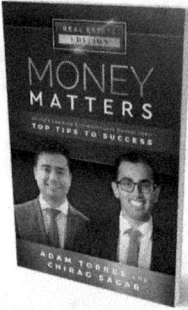

Navigating the world of real estate can be stressful. Are you getting closer or further from your goals? Finance guru Adam Torres is here to help you move forward. His guide, Money Matters, features 15 top professionals who share lessons from their more than 250 years of combined experience.

Purchase at **MoneyMattersTopTips.com/store**

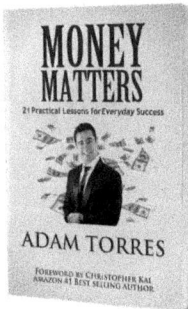

In this clear, concise manual, financial expert Adam Torres goes over the basics of personal finance and investing and shows you how to grow your wealth. Torres makes sure you are prepared for whatever life throws your way. It's never too early to think about the future and his book will give you the right tools to tackle it.

Purchase at **MoneyMattersTopTips.com/store** or listen to the audiobook version FREE on YouTube at Ask Adam Torres

OTHER AVAILABLE TITLES

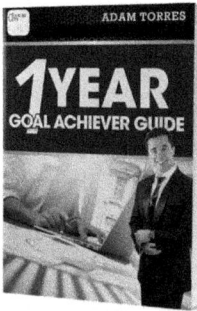

This workbook has been designed specifically for individuals like you who are dedicated to improving the results in all areas of their lives! By following the ideas and exercises presented to you in this transformational workbook, you are automatically moving yourself into the realm of top achievers worldwide.

Download FREE at **MoneyMattersTopTips.com/store**

WORK CITED

"Actors | Data USA." https://datausa.io/profile/soc/272011/. Accessed 5 Sep. 2018.

"Hollywood Equality: All Talk, Little Action | USC Annenberg School for ...." https://annenberg.usc.edu/news/faculty-research/hollywood-equality-all-talk-little-action. Accessed 5 Sep. 2018.

"Research – Center for the Study of Women in Television & Film." https://womenintvfilm.sdsu.edu/research/. Accessed 5 Sep. 2018.

"Hollywood Equality: All Talk, Little Action | USC Annenberg School for ...." https://annenberg.usc.edu/news/faculty-research/hollywood-equality-all-talk-little-action. Accessed 6 Sep. 2018.

"'Crazy Rich Asians' Broke More Box Office Records During Labor Day ...." 4 Sep. 2018, https://www.huffingtonpost.com/entry/crazy-rich-asians-labor-day-box-office_us_5b8e7d1ae4b0cf7b00399291. Accessed 6 Sep. 2018.

"'Crazy Rich Asians' Becomes Most Successful Studio Rom-Com in 9 ...." 3 Sep. 2018, https://www.hollywoodreporter.com/news/crazy-rich-asians-becomes-successful-studio-rom-9-years-at-us-box-office-1139353. Accessed 6 Sep. 2018.

"Slumdog Millionaire - Awards - IMDb." https://www.imdb.com/title/tt1010048/awards. Accessed 6 Sep. 2018.

"2018 Hollywood Diversity report - Social Sciences." 26 Feb. 2018, https://socialsciences.ucla.edu/wp-content/uploads/2018/02/UCLA-Hollywood-Diversity-Report-2018-2-27-18.pdf. Accessed 7 Sep. 2018.

www.ingramcontent.com/pod-product-compliance
Lightning Source LLC
Chambersburg PA
CBHW060900280326
41934CB00007B/1133